really easy bidding

Really Easy Bidding is for people who can recognise a pack of cards and now want to do something entertaining with them.

Bridge for All – the complete Learn and Play programme from the English Bridge Union – has developed a simple bidding system for beginners called Standard English. Derived from the widely played Acol system, the most popular system played in England and many other countries too, Standard English sorts out the areas where opinions differ.

Based on the weak no trump opening and a minimum of conventions, the Foundation version of Standard English is the ideal starting point for those learning to bid correctly. Armed with this knowledge the reader will be able to face bridge players anywhere in England, confident that their bids will be readily understood.

Enjoy the book, then go out and enjoy playing bridge.

Sandra Landy
Series Editor

The English Bridge Union
Broadfields,
Bicester Road
Aylesbury HP19 3BG
Tel: 01296 317217
Fax: 01296 317220
Email: bfa@ebu.co.uk

Really Easy
Bidding

The English Bridge Union

First Published by the English Bridge Union in England in 1998.
Second edition 1999

© English Bridge Union Ltd 1998

ISBN 0 9506279 2 5

Designed by Milestone Strategic Creative Design of Beaconsfield

Typeset by Wakewing of High Wycombe

Printed and bound by Polestar Wheatons of Exeter

contents

the really easy bridge series

what is the aim of the series?

The Really Easy Bridge Series presents the fundamentals of the game in a clear usable way. The reader will be able to put the ideas into practice in their very next game. It is not for the expert or those who enjoy learned discussions on theory.

who is it for?

- People who can play MiniBridge and want to progress to bridge proper
- Students in bridge classes who want to supplement the teaching notes
- Those wishing to update their game with modern methods of bidding

how to use the books

- Bridge is a partnership game – read this book with your partner and you will both benefit twice as much.
- Try the quizzes when you've read each chapter but go back later and try them again.
- Play bridge. Practice makes perfect.

Really Easy Play in No Trumps is now available and watch out for other titles on the subjects of play with trumps, defence and further details of the Standard English System.

introduction

What is bridge? Bridge is a card game.

Bridge is fun!

It is played worldwide by more than fifty million people. Some play at home, others in a club. For some the social contact is the main attraction, for others it is the competition and pitting of wits that gets the adrenalin flowing.

Bridge can be as relaxed as you want. No one has to be an expert to enjoy it. Many of the keenest participants have no ambition to be world beaters. However, it is an intellectual game and can be played with great skill. Once involved, many players make every effort to improve and develop their game to the limit of their ability.

So how do you start? Go to a bridge class, run by a qualified bridge teacher. You will be taught the fundamentals of the game, and introduced to competitive bridge. The ENGLISH BRIDGE UNION has looked after bridge in England since 1936.

It has developed a system by which competent bridge teachers follow a nationally accredited course. If you are taught by a teacher using the English Bridge Union's BRIDGE FOR ALL scheme you can feel confident that you will be well taught, and that what you learn will enable you to turn up at a new bridge club and be on the same wavelength as a partner you have never met before.

Ring the English Bridge Union at Aylesbury and ask about *Bridge for All*. The number is 01296 317217. You will get a warm welcome and further information.

1 the objective of bridge

So what is the idea of bridge? It is a game for four players, who sit around a square table. For convenience they are described by the compass points, as shown below:

North

West East

South

East and West are partners, playing on the same side. Equally North and South are playing together. They play with a pack of 52 cards.

The pack has four suits: spades (♠), hearts (♥), diamonds (♦) and clubs (♣). Each suit has thirteen cards, in order of importance they are: ace, king, queen, jack, 10, 9, 8, 7, 6, 5, 4, 3, 2

The 52 cards in the pack are divided between the four players, each having thirteen. All the players are allowed to look at their own cards, but not those of anybody else. By means of an auction (which will be described in chapter 2) one of the sides makes a promise, or CONTRACT to make a specific number of tricks. A trick consists of one card from each of the four players, with the highest card winning the trick – all will be clear by the end of the chapter.

The promises are themselves said in code. A contract of one no trump (1NT) by one side promises that the partners will win at least seven tricks. Because there are thirteen tricks and anybody winning the contract has to take more than half we don't count the first six.

A contract of six no trumps (6NT) promises to make twelve tricks. You must be pretty confident to try that because it only allows you to lose one of the thirteen tricks. A contract of four hearts (4 ♥) promises to make ten tricks, but now the heart suit becomes special, called a trump suit. Even the lowliest two of hearts is more powerful than any card of any other suit.

If you succeed in your contract you score points. The more you promise to make, the more points you score, provided you succeed!

Firstly, there is the trick score which depends on what is trumps.

NT no trumps 40 for the first and 30 for subsequent tricks

♠ spades   ♥ hearts 30 per trick (these are the MAJORS)

♦ diamonds ♣ clubs   20 per trick (these are the MINORS)

Secondly, there is a bonus for making a contract.

If your trick score comes to at least 100 you are said to be in a GAME contract – bonus is 300

If your trick score comes to less than 100 you are said to be in a PART SCORE contract – bonus is 50.

Finally, if you promise to make twelve or thirteen tricks you score an extra bonus.

Contracting to make twelve tricks is called a SMALL SLAM – bonus is 500.

Contracting to make thirteen tricks is called a GRAND SLAM – bonus is 1000.

What if you fail to keep your promise? You get absolutely nothing! For each trick by which you fail (called an UNDERTRICK) your opponents score 50 points.

Now you can see the dilemma you face. If you contract to make a low number of tricks but make many more, you are sure of scoring points, but not many! The big bonuses that you could

You don't have to learn the scores by heart

have enjoyed elude you. On the other hand, if you promise to make lots of tricks and fail, you score nothing at all. It is very frustrating to make twelve out of the thirteen available tricks and actually have to concede 50 points to your opponents. The skill of bidding is being able to forecast how many tricks you will make.

scoring table, not vulnerable

Contract	Trick score	Part-score or game bonus	Slam bonus	Total
1 club/diamond	20	50		70
1 heart/spade	30	50		80
1 no trump	40	50		90
2 clubs/diamonds	40	50		90
2 hearts/spades	60	50		110
2 no trumps	70	50		120
3 clubs/diamonds	60	50		110
3 hearts/spades	90	50		140
3 no trumps	100	300		400
4 clubs/diamonds	80	50		130
4 hearts/spades	120	300		420
4 no trumps	130	300		430
5 clubs/diamonds	100	300		400
5 hearts/spades	150	300		450
5 no trumps	160	300		460
6 clubs/diamonds	120	300	500	920
6 hearts/spades	180	300	500	980
6 no trumps	190	300	500	990
7 clubs/diamonds	140	300	1000	1440
7 hearts/spades	210	300	1000	1510
7 no trumps	220	300	1000	1520

Score for each extra trick, or OVERTRICK, 20 in a minor and 30 in a major or no trumps.

scoring table, vulnerable

Contract	Trick score	Part-score or game bonus	Slam bonus	Total
1 club/diamond	20	50		70
1 heart/spade	30	50		80
1 no trump	40	50		90
2 clubs/diamonds	40	50		90
2 hearts/spades	60	50		110
2 no trumps	70	50		120
3 clubs/diamonds	60	50		110
3 hearts/spades	90	50		140
3 no trumps	100	500		600
4 clubs/diamonds	80	50		130
4 hearts/spades	120	500		620
4 no trumps	130	500		630
5 clubs/diamonds	100	500		600
5 hearts/spades	150	500		650
5 no trumps	160	500		660
6 clubs/diamonds	120	500	750	1370
6 hearts/spades	180	500	750	1430
6 no trumps	190	500	750	1440
7 clubs/diamonds	140	500	1500	2140
7 hearts/spades	210	500	1500	2210
7 no trumps	220	500	1500	2220

Score for each extra trick, or overtrick, 20 in a minor and 30 in a major or no trumps.

Half the time a different table of scoring applies. For the table on page 4 you are said to be NOT VULNERABLE, but for the table above you are VULNERABLE. You can see that the game and slam bonuses are higher. So you can score more heavily, but if you fail the penalties are greater – each undertrick concedes 100 points to the opponents.

After attending a bridge class for a while, your teacher might introduce you to a simple duplicate competition. Let us follow the fortunes of John and Claire. They sit North and South and they are told they are pair number 3. Their East/West opponents are pair number 7. The tutor brings them two plastic boards. In it, there are four slots, labelled North, South, East and West, and each has thirteen cards. The players take out the cards from the slot corresponding to their direction and each player looks at his own cards.

As a result of the bidding, Claire, who is South, buys the contract in three no trumps (3NT). The battle lines are drawn. The board tells them that if North/South have the contract they will be not vulnerable, while if East/West buy the contract they will be vulnerable. If Claire makes at least nine tricks she fulfils her contract and scores at least 400 points. If she makes eight tricks she scores nothing and concedes 50 points to the opposition.

Claire occupies a special role. She is called the DECLARER. She has special responsibilities, and the special privilege that she will be allowed to see John's hand and actually tell him which cards to play. John's involvement in this deal is virtually over. He will be the DUMMY.

Everything in bridge happens in a clockwise direction, so because the South hand is declarer, the hand sitting after declarer, West, plays the first card. Then the dummy is placed face up on the table and everybody can see it. In the picture you are shown all four hands. At the table the players only see dummy and their own hand.

It doesn't matter if you make a mistake – everybody else does

```
                    ♠ 7 6
                    ♥ 9 8 4
                    ♦ A Q J 2
                    ♣ 7 6 5 2
    ♠ J 5 4 3      ┌─────────┐      ♠ A K Q
    ♥ 10 3 2       │    N    │      ♥ J 7 6 5
    ♦ 5 4 3        │ W     E │      ♦ 10 9 8 6
    ♣ Q 9 8        │    S    │      ♣ J 10
                   └─────────┘
                    ♠ 10 9 8 2
                    ♥ A K Q
                    ♦ K 7
                    ♣ A K 4 3
```

The card West chose to play first, called the OPENING LEAD, is
the ♠3. Claire tells dummy to play the ♠6. Because a spade was
led, each hand must play a spade if it has one. East decides to
play the ♠Q and South the ♠2. These four cards form the first
trick. It is won by the highest card, which is East's ♠Q.

Each player puts the card he has just played face down on the table
in front of him. The partnership of East/West won the trick, so they
put their cards pointing towards them. North/South put their cards
parallel with their edge of the table because they lost the trick.

From the partner's point of view it doesn't matter whether East or
West win the trick, they are on the same side. However, since
East won the trick it is East who must play first to the next trick. At
trick 2 East tries the ♠A. South plays the ♠8, East the ♠4 and
North (as instructed by Claire) the ♠7.

Having won trick two East leads to trick three, continuing with the
♠K. This wins the trick, South following with the ♠9 and East the
♠5. North doesn't have any spades left so South can tell him to
play any card she chooses. South tells North to throw away
(discard) a card that seems worthless, the ♣2.

Having no spades left, East must try something else at trick 4 and
switches to the ♥5. South wins the trick with the ♥A. For the first

time North and South can put their cards pointing towards them. The table now looks like this:

South now wins trick 5 with the ♦K, enters dummy with the ♦A at trick six and wins tricks seven and eight with the ♦Q and ♦J, discarding useless clubs from her hand. The next four tricks are won in the South hand with the ♥K, ♥Q, ♣A and ♣K but she loses the last trick to West's ♠J.

Nine of the thirteen cards in front of her are pointing towards her, so Claire knows she has won nine tricks, fulfilling her contract. The four players put the cards back in the correct slots. They calculate the score. North/South are entitled to 300 for bidding and making the game of 3NT, plus 100 for the trick score. That comes to 400. This score is entered on a piece of paper that comes with the board (called a TRAVELLER). Later the hand will be played by other players at other tables.

At the end of the evening the tutor takes the travellers and works out something called MATCH POINTS. There were eight pairs playing. Everybody played the board, four pairs as North/South and four pairs as East/West. After the tutor had finished scoring, Claire and John looked at the traveller.

SECTION   BOARD NUMBER 3

PAIRS NS	No. EW	Contract and Result	Tricks	By	NORTH-SOUTH Plus	NORTH-SOUTH Minus	Match	Point
3	7	3NT ✓	9	S	400		5	1
4	5	3NT − 1	8	S		50	0	6
6	1	3NT ✓	9	S	400		5	1
8	2	2NT +1	9	S	150		2	4

They were curious about the other results. It seemed that pair 4 had failed to make 3NT. It transpired that the first four tricks were identical. However, declarer then made the mistake of cashing dummy's ♦A at trick five and winning trick six in his hand with the ♦K. Now he couldn't ever score tricks with the ♦Q and ♦J because there were no further entries to dummy.

Finally, pair 8 had been more cautious in the bidding, only contracting for eight tricks in 2NT. They made an overtrick.

How about the curious entries made by the tutor under the heading: MATCH POINTS. Apparently, he compared the scores of all the pairs who played with the North/South cards. The most successful North/South pair were numbers 3 and 6 who scored +400. They beat two other North/South pairs, numbers 4 and 8, and tied with each other. They were each awarded 5 match points, two for each pair beaten and one for tying with each other. Pair 8 scored 2 match points for beating pair 4.

We now return to earlier in the evening. Having finished playing board 3, they started to play board 4. This time both sides were vulnerable. Claire and John decided that they had better be cautious in the bidding, and since they had poor cards, at no time did they suggest they might make a contract. However, their East/West opponents seemed to be enjoying themselves and settled for a contract of 7♦. They had to make all thirteen tricks.

Here is the deal.

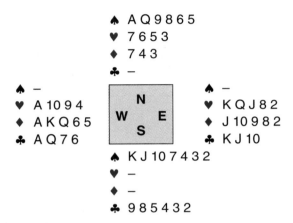

The declarer was West so John, as North, had to lead the first card. Feeling optimistic, he tried leading the ♠A. East put his hand face up on the table as dummy, and was seen to have no spades. Declarer instructed East to play the ♦2. South had to contribute a spade (the suit led) and declarer discarded the ♣6 from his hand.

So which card won the trick? Remember, the contract was 7♦. For this deal diamonds are a special suit, called trumps. If you can legally play a diamond it beats any other card of any other suit, so dummy's humble ♦2 won the trick.

Declarer proceeded to play enough diamonds to make sure North had none left (called DRAWING TRUMPS) and then continued by cashing lots of high cards in clubs and hearts. There was nothing John or Claire could do except congratulate their opponents. It occurred to Claire that it was a good job for declarer that he had chosen a contract with a trump suit of diamonds, otherwise if there had been no trumps the defenders could have helped themselves to an awful lot of spade tricks. The East/West score was computed from the vulnerable table to be 2140, and this was entered on the traveller. Then the two pairs thanked each other, wished each other good luck for the remainder of the evening, and moved to new tables where they played new boards against different opponents.

Here was the traveller for board 4 at the end of the competition.

PAIRS NS	No. EW	Contract and Result	Tricks	By	NORTH-SOUTH		Match	Points
					Plus	Minus		
3	7	7D /	13	W		2140	0	6
4	5	7Sx /	13	S	2470		6	0
6	1	6S+1	13	W		1390	3	3
8	2	6S+1	13	W		1390	3	3

SECTION   BOARD NUMBER 4

Claire and John saw that they had no match points at all for this hand. They felt unlucky because their opponents had tried the ambitious contract of 7♦. Pairs 6 and 8 had contracted for only 6♦, making an overtrick. They scored 3 points each: 2 for beating pair 3 and 1 for tying with each other.

The other score fascinated Claire and John. It seems that pair 4 had contracted as North/South to make all thirteen tricks with spades as trumps. The opponents had been confident they would fail, and doubled their contract to increase the penalty. (You will learn about doubles in chapter 2.) However, North/South had made all thirteen tricks.

Apparently, pair 4 had bid 7♠, not because they expected to make it, but because the confidence of East/West in contracting for a grand slam was so impressive that it seemed certain to make. North and South had both suggested they might try a spade contract, and South felt they would concede fewer points by buying their own contract in spades. The result was sensational!

South was declarer, so West made the opening lead, the ♦A. Dummy was put face up on the table and on the fourth card to the trick South, with no diamonds, had played a trump (spade) to win the trick. At trick 2 South started with the ♣2 and called for a trump from dummy. At trick 3 dummy's ♥3 was trumped by South's ♠3. Backwards and forwards went declarer, trumping (or RUFFING) clubs in dummy and the red suits in his hand. When the smoke finally cleared declarer had made all thirteen tricks. Try it by setting up the hands from a real pack! Claire and John reflected on the awesome power of trumps, which sometimes seem to have as much influence on the outcome as aces and kings.

At the end of the evening they had played eight hands. The total match points they scored over all eight boards left them in third place out of eight. A tiring, but most enjoyable experience.

Don't forget to smile at your partner – it shows you're enjoying yourself

2 the code of bidding

In chapter 1 you were often told that one of the sides had mysteriously ended up with a contract to make a number of tricks with or without a trump suit. Clearly, something had happened before the opening lead was made to arrive at this position. It is an auction.

When the deal is complete, the auction starts and the dealer is the first player to make a bid. Then everybody else has a chance to bid, in clockwise rotation.

As in any other auction, you don't have to bid or you can start with as low a bid as you wish, but if anybody wants to compete with your bid, he must make a higher one. Those available are, starting with 1♣ as the lowest:

7 level	7♣, 7♦, 7♥, 7♠, 7NT
6 level	6♣, 6♦, 6♥, 6♠, 6NT
5 level	5♣, 5♦, 5♥, 5♠, 5NT
4 level	4♣, 4♦, 4♥, 4♠, 4NT
3 level	3♣, 3♦, 3♥, 3♠, 3NT
2 level	2♣, 2♦, 2♥, 2♠, 2NT
1 level	1♣, 1♦, 1♥, 1♠, 1NT

Note that clubs is the cheapest suit, followed by diamonds. The minor suits score only 20 per trick, so they really are the poor relations. Next up come the major suits: hearts and spades. Higher in ranking and scoring 30 per trick, they have greater importance. Sitting on top of the status scale is no trumps: 40 for the first trick and 30 for each one after that.

The best way to learn what happens in an auction is to see some unfold.

West	North	East	South
pass	pass	pass	pass

This is the simplest of auctions. West is dealer, and declines to bid. He says 'pass'. Each other player makes the same decision. The four consecutive passes end the auction and that is the end of that hand.

West	North	East	South
1 ♥	pass	1 ♠	pass
2 ♦	pass	2 ♥	pass
pass	pass		

West deals and suggests hearts might be trumps by bidding 1 ♥. This is the OPENING BID. It shows his longest suit is hearts.

North doesn't want to make a bid. He passes.

1 ♠ is a higher bid than 1 ♥ so East can make this bid (called a RESPONSE). It shows at least four spades and the message is that maybe spades rather than hearts will make the best trump suit. A trump suit is acceptable if in the combined hands you hold at least eight of the thirteen cards in a suit. If East had four hearts in his hand, he would settle for hearts as trumps.

South passes, showing no desire to bid.

West wants to make a second bid (or REBID) in diamonds, but because 1 ♦ is a cheaper bid than 1 ♠, if he wants to suggest diamonds he must bid 2 ♦. North passes again.

East could pass 2♦ to play with diamonds as trumps but to make hearts trumps he bids 2♥. East is giving preference to West's longest suit and he won't have four hearts – if he had, he would have supported hearts last time.

The other three players have a chance to bid but choose not to do so. 2♥ is the final contract and West is declarer. East's 2♥ bid won the auction but West is declarer because hearts are trumps and declarer is always the first player of the partnership that won the contract to bid the DENOMINATION (i.e. suit or no trumps). North makes the opening lead, East's hand becomes the dummy, and West tries to make at least eight tricks with hearts as trumps.

You will see by now that these bids are really like holding a conversation. It says:

West: I like hearts.

East: I am not convinced it is right to play in hearts – how about spades?

West: I am not happy about spades – how about diamonds?

East: I give in. I prefer hearts to diamonds.

West	North	East	South
		1♠	pass
2♠	pass	4♠	pass
pass	pass		

East is dealer and opens 1♠. West is obviously happy with spades and raises East's suit. If you study the scoring you will see that a contract of 2♠ hardly scores better than 1♠, so why contract for eight tricks rather than seven?

The answer is that West knows there is a chance of the game bonus if East has something extra and can bid 4♠. East accepts the challenge and the final three passes close the auction. Note that East is perfectly entitled to jump a level of bidding if he chooses.

West	North	East	South
		1♥	1♠
2♥	2♠	3♥	3♠
pass	pass	pass	

This auction features both sides bidding, what we call a competitive auction. Each side is prepared to push the bidding higher in order to impose its own trump suit. For example, East's 3♥ bid promises to make nine tricks with hearts as trumps. South chooses to bid 3♠ with a target of nine tricks because he thinks he'll get a better score. Outbidding the opponents at a high level isn't silly. You saw in chapter 1 an example of a hand in which each side could make all thirteen tricks provided they picked the trump suit.

Two reasons for the bidding to reach a higher level.

■ Getting the game bonus.

■ The two opposing sides are trying to pick the trump suit.

However, how do you know when to stop? How did North/South decide there was the potential for nine tricks? How did East/West know they should play in a part-score rather than game? In the early years of bridge even the best players in the world bid until they felt like stopping. This led to some haphazard contracts. Then the best brains started to look for a little more precision. Even with just thirteen words available (pass, the numbers 1 to 7, no trumps, spades, hearts, diamonds and clubs), only usable in specific combinations, it was possible to do far better. Their conclusions revolutionised bidding:

■ It is possible to put a numerical value on a hand, rather than just feel: 'This looks a nice hand,' or 'This is a load of rubbish.' It is called the point count. We count an ace as four points, a king as three, a queen as two and a jack as one. There are 10 points in each suit and 40 in the pack. Note that these points (HIGH CARD POINTS or HCP) are different from the scoring points seen earlier.

- To have a reasonable chance of making a game contract you and your partner normally need at least 25 and preferably 26 of the 40 points between your two hands. Equally, if you have to contract for a minor suit, requiring eleven tricks for game, you may need as many as 28; 33 points are normally required for a small slam (twelve tricks).

- Long suits are worth tricks, particularly if they are trumps. After all, if you have all thirteen spades in your hand you can underwrite a contract of 7♠, yet the point count is only 10. You can make a game contract with fewer than the normal number of points if you have long suits.

- It is possible to give much more precise meanings to the bids. We can treat them as a code, with agreement between the partners on the key to the code. This is called a SYSTEM. Of course all four players understand the code. For example, your system may include the agreement that an opening bid of 1NT shows 12, 13 or 14 points in a hand with no long suits. Armed with that precise knowledge your partner should know what to do.

The most commonly played system in Great Britain is called ACOL. It was invented in 1934 by four eminent players in a house in Acol Road in London. However, it has changed over the years, and different players have different ideas of what constitutes Acol. So the English Bridge Union has taken a commonly played version of Acol and called it STANDARD ENGLISH. If you are taught bridge under the *Bridge for All* scheme you will be taught Standard English, giving you a universal bidding language.

Finally, how do you deal with opponents who consistently bid more than they can make, perhaps competing over your reasonable contract to make a contract that fails by plenty? When it is your turn to call you can say DOUBLE if the last bid was made by one of your opponents. Look at this:

West	North	East	South
1♥	3♠	dbl	pass
pass	pass		

East's double says 'I don't think 3♠ will make nine tricks'.

Doubling has a dramatic effect on the score.

Suppose North makes nine tricks in 3♠ doubled and nobody is vulnerable. Firstly, the trick score is doubled, making 180 (rather than 90). This in turn means that the trick score comes to more than 100, so the game bonus of 300 applies rather than the part-score bonus of 50. In addition, North is given an extra 50 points, called 'for the insult' 180 + 300 + 50 = 530.

Overtricks count for more in a doubled contract. Usually an overtrick in spades would be 30 points, but doubled it becomes 100 non-vulnerable or 200 vulnerable. Incidentally, doubling 3♠ creates a game contract, but doesn't create a slam.

On the other hand, what if North fails in 3♠ doubled? The penalty is severe and is given in the table below:

	Non-vulnerable	Vulnerable
One undertrick	100	200
Two undertricks	300	500
Three undertricks	500	800
For more undertricks, keep adding on 300		

Now you can see why it doesn't pay to make silly bids to stop your opponents making their contract.

What if the enemy double your contract, or your partner's contract and you believe they are wrong? You can REDOUBLE at your turn, for example:

West	North	East	South
1NT	pass	3NT	dbl
pass	pass	redbl	pass
pass	pass		

South thinks 3NT will fail. East disagrees. The stakes are high!

Redoubling doubles again all trick scores, so 3NT redoubled scores 100 x 2 x 2 = 400 and there is the game bonus. The 'insult' bonus doubles up from 50 to 100. In total that makes 800 not vulnerable or 1000 vulnerable. Redoubled overtricks score double the score for doubled overtricks.

On the other hand, if the contract fails all the scores in the table of doubled undertricks are doubled again. This could be an expensive business for somebody.

At this stage a little reassurance is necessary – you will probably only play one or two redoubled contracts in your life! You certainly don't need to remember the scores.

Finally, a few words on the ethics of the game. Bridge is a game of communicating with your partner. How do you do this? By making bids and playing cards. Not through facial expressions and tone of voice. Of course, this is a counsel of perfection. If your partner is clearly unhappy at how things are progressing it can be hard not to realise it, particularly if you are a partnership in life as well as bridge! You can only do your best to ignore it. Equally, you must try to keep a serene temperament, never criticising your partner or opponents. That way everybody enjoys the game.

What if something goes wrong? For example, you make an illegal bid like bidding 1 ♥ over 1 ♠, or don't follow suit when you could have done. We all do it at times. The person in charge (called the DIRECTOR, or it might be your teacher) will sort it out. The laws of the game tell him what to do. No blame is attached and no hard feelings. Have a good laugh about it.

The laws are there to put things right when something goes wrong.

3 opening 1NT

Bridge players love jargon. It can be rather off-putting to those who are not used to it, but most of it really isn't difficult to understand. What do you think it means if you overhear someone describing a hand as a '4-4-3-2 16 count'?

4-4-3-2 refers to the SHAPE of the hand. There are two suits with four cards each, a suit with three cards and a suit with only two cards (called a DOUBLETON). 4+4+3+2 comes to thirteen, the total number of cards in the hand. The term '16 count' says it has 16 high card points. Actually, the phrase describes the main features of the hand rather well, doesn't it?

Some hands have roughly the same number of cards in each suit. They are called BALANCED hands. Hands with 4-3-3-3 or 4-4-3-2 shape are balanced. Your reaction on picking up a balanced hand is that there may be no special reason to have a trump suit, particularly because no trumps scores higher.

Other hands have long and short suits. These are called UNBALANCED. For example, suppose you are dealt a 6-6-1-0 hand: two 6-card suits, a suit with only one card (called a SINGLETON) and a suit in which you have no cards at all (called a VOID). You will take some persuading that one of your long suits shouldn't be trumps. With an unbalanced hand you will spend the early part of the auction telling partner about your suits, hoping he likes them.

The most common unbalanced shapes are: 5-4-3-1, 5-4-2-2 and 4-4-4-1.

Depending on whether your hand is balanced or unbalanced, you describe it to your partner in the auction in a very different way.

With a balanced hand, you are anxious to bid no trumps early. A balanced hand doesn't contain a singleton or void, and it has at most one doubleton.

5-3-3-2 shape hands are common enough. It is sensible to treat them as balanced if your 5-card suit is a minor, but if you hold a 5-card major you should start by bidding it. This demonstrates the different priority between major and minor suits. You give high priority to finding out if you have an 8-card major suit fit and making it trumps. If you have an 8-card minor suit fit you often prefer a contract in no trumps because it can be such a struggle to make eleven tricks for a minor suit game.

In chapter 2 you were told that you tend to need 25 or 26 points to make playing a game contract reasonable. It would clearly be a shame if such values were present for your partnership but neither of you made a bid, so you really must make an opening bid if you are dealt 13 points (half of 26). Sometimes you will open with 12 points.

We now look at some balanced hands. How suitable do you think they are for opening one no trump?

♠ A Q 8 6 ♥ K 6 ♦ J 7 5 4 ♣ K 8 6	This hand is very suitable. It is 4-4-3-2 shape with 13 points. It has at least one high card in every suit. Open 1NT.
♠ A Q 8 6 ♥ K 6 ♦ K J 5 4 ♣ 8 7 6	This is also a 4-4-3-2 shape and 13 points. It is correct to open 1NT. This tells partner that your hand is balanced and has 12 to 14 points, a very helpful message.

♠ A Q 8 ♥ K 6 ♦ 8 7 6 ♣ K J 5 4 3	This is also a 1NT opening bid, a 5-3-3-2 shape hand with 13 points. Because the 5-card suit is a minor, the hand is opened 1NT.
♠ A Q 6 ♥ K 6 2 ♦ A 7 6 2 ♣ A 6 5	This one seems very suitable for 1NT, but it isn't! Just because a hand may seem suitable doesn't mean that you can start by bidding no trumps. The 1NT opening is a very special bid.

A 1NT OPENING BID SHOWS 12-14 POINTS, A BALANCED HAND WITH NO 5-CARD MAJOR.

It is called a LIMIT BID. That means that its strength is very closely defined, or limited.

Look back at the last hand. It is outside the range of 12-14 points. With 17 points it is too strong for a 1NT opening bid. Neither is it suitable to open 2NT (another coded limit bid) or indeed any number of no trumps. You will have to bid your only 4-card suit, diamonds. You will learn that a 1♦ opening bid is not a limit bid, and can be as weak as 12 points or as strong as 19 points.

The 1NT opening bid tells a lot of the story. Responder is in charge of steering the partnership to the correct final contract. He adds his points to the points shown by opener and uses common sense, guided by the following principles:

If there are clearly not the values for game present, responder arranges for the auction to end as soon as possible. He might pass, or he might make a bid which tells partner unconditionally to pass, called a SIGN-OFF bid.

♠ A 8 5 ♥ K 7 4 ♦ 10 7 5 4 ♣ Q 6 5	Responder has 9 points and opposite a 12-14 1NT the maximum combined strength is 23 points. It is right to pass.

If values for game are present and the denomination (suit or no trumps) is clear, responder bids the appropriate game. Opener must pass, so these are also sign-off bids.

♠ A 8 5	Adding responder's 14 points to opener's
♥ K 7 4	12-14 gives the partnership a combined total
♦ K 10 7 4	of 26-28 points. It is right to bid 3NT.
♣ A 6 5	

♠ A J 5	There is enough for game. You have six
♥ A J 9 4 3 2	hearts and partner has guaranteed at least
♦ K 10 7	two with the 1NT opening. With at least an
♣ 7	8-card fit in hearts, bid 4♥.

♠ A J 5	Wherever possible you play in no trumps
♥ 7 4	rather than a minor suit. You don't have
♦ K 10 7	enough points to consider a contract of 5♣.
♣ A J 9 3 2	Just bid 3NT.

If the values for game might or might not be present, depending on whether opener has minimum or maximum values for 1NT, responder makes an INVITATIONAL bid. Opener is free to pass if minimum, but is invited to bid again if maximum.

♠ A 8 5	Here responder has 12 points. If opener has
♥ K 7 4	12 the combined total is 24, not enough for
♦ J 10 7 4	3NT. If opener has 14 the total is 26.
♣ A 6 5	Responder bids 2NT, inviting opener to pass
	with 12 and bid 3NT with 14 points. With 13
	points opener decides, with a couple of tens
	or a 5-card suit, he would bid 3NT.

Sometimes the values for game are definitely present but you are not sure which game will be best. You can make a bid which asks partner's opinion. Because it forces opener to bid again it is called a FORCING bid.

♠ A J 5
♥ A J 9 3 2
♦ K 10 7
♣ 7 4

The values for game are present, but which game? You want to play in 3NT if partner has just two hearts, or 4♥ otherwise. You can ask partner this question by jumping to 3♥. This bid is forcing. Opener MUST bid, either 3NT with just two hearts or 4♥ with longer hearts. When you have a 5-card major suit it is worth investigating alternatives to 3NT, but don't bother with a 5-card minor.

2♦, 2♥ and 2♠ over 1NT are weak bids. Partner must pass.

♠ 9 8 5
♥ Q 8 7 5 4 3
♦ 9 6 4
♣ 7

♠ A 8 5
♥ Q 8 7 5 4
♦ 9 6 4 3
♣ 7

These two hands demonstrate the first principle. Values for game are not present, but responder would prefer to play in hearts rather than no trumps. In 1NT, partner might lose a lot of club tricks. With hearts as trumps you can trump the second club. Trumps act as a sort of stopper. You sign off in 2♥.

We have already seen the desirability of finding and playing in an 8-card fit in a major suit. Often responder will have a 4-card major suit and feel that if opener also has four cards in the same major suit, that should be the trump suit. How can he find out?

You have already seen that bids are codes. So far the codes have also shown length in the suit bid, or a balanced hand if no trumps was bid. However it is sometimes sensible to use bids in a coded manner that says nothing about the suit bid. Such a bid is called a CONVENTION. Conventions are frequently named after the player who invented them, and one of the most useful and widely played is called the STAYMAN convention.

In response to 1NT, 2♣ says nothing about clubs, but asks opener: 'Have you got a 4-card major suit?'

Opener must rebid as follows:

2♦ says, 'Sorry, I don't have a 4-card major suit.'

2♥ says, 'I have four hearts. I might also have four spades.'

2♠ says, 'I have four spades but I don't have four hearts.'

> To use Stayman responder must hold a 4-card major and be prepared for any reply from partner. The exception is a weak hand with long clubs. Responder starts with 2♣ and over any of opener's rebids, bids 3♣. This is a sign-off bid and is the only way to play in a part-score in clubs.

♠ 2	South	North
♥ 3 2	1NT	2♣
♦ Q J 9	2♦/♥/♠	3♣
♣ Q 9 8 7 6 5 4	pass	

So can responder safely use Stayman with these hands if his partner opens 1NT?

I'm responder – I'm in charge!

♠ A J 7 4	Yes, he bids 2♣. If opener rebids
♥ K 9 8	2♦ or 2♥, responder continues with
♦ 7 5	3NT. If opener rebids 2♠, responder
♣ A Q 5 4	jumps to 4♠.

♠ A J 7 4	Yes, bid 2♣. If opener bids 2♦ or 2♥,
♥ K 9 8	responder continues with 2NT, invitational
♦ 7 5	showing 11-12 points. If opener bids 2♠,
♣ K 10 8 7	responder invites with 3♠.

♠ 8	No, he must pass. If he bids 2♣ he would be
♥ A J 7 4	in trouble over a 2♠ rebid. Remember, a 2NT
♦ 10 7 6 5	continuation shows 11-12 points.
♣ K 8 6 5	

♠ Q 8 6 5 4	Yes, bid 2♣. Over 2♥ or 2♠, pass. Over 2♦,
♥ K 7 4 3	sign off in 2♠. This is a rare example of a
♦ 7 4	hand with no prospect of game being suitable
♣ J 8	for Stayman.

The Stayman 2♣ convention asks opener questions, but its use also conveys information and opener must keep his wits about him. How should he continue after the sequence below?

South	North
1NT	2♣ (Stayman)
2♥	2NT
?	

♠ A Q 7 2
♥ K J 4 3
♦ 10 7 5
♣ A 7

South knows North has 11-12 points and a 4-card major. As North doesn't like hearts, he must have spades. A 4-4 spade fit exists and South must bid it. With a maximum 1NT, bid 4♠.

♠ A 7 6 2
♥ K J 4 3
♦ 10 7 5
♣ A 7

South has a minimum 1NT. He signs off in 3♠.

There is a quiz on the next page. Cover the right-hand column so you can't see the answers. Try the questions THEN look at the answers.

quiz on chapter 3

Your partner opens 1NT. What do you respond with these hands?

♠ K 10 8 7 6 2 ♥ 7 ♦ K J 7 ♣ 9 7 5	2♠. A sign-off. 2♠ will be the final contract.
♠ K 10 8 7 6 2 ♥ 7 ♦ K Q 7 ♣ A 7 5	4♠. A sign-off. This time values for game are there.
♠ K 10 8 7 2 ♥ A 4 ♦ A K 8 ♣ 6 4 3	3♠. Forcing. Opener will raise to 4♠ with three or four spades or rebid 3NT otherwise.
♠ A Q 4 ♥ 8 4 ♦ K 9 7 6 ♣ J 7 5 4	Pass. Not enough values for game.
♠ A Q 4 2 ♥ 8 4 ♦ K 8 4 3 ♣ J 4 3	Pass. Don't use Stayman. 2♥ or 2♦ will leave you stuck, since now 2NT shows 11-12 points.
♠ A Q 4 ♥ K 4 ♦ K 9 7 6 ♣ J 10 7 5	3NT. A sign-off. At least 25 points between the hands.
♠ A Q 4 2 ♥ K 4 ♦ K 8 4 3 ♣ J 10 3	2♣. Stayman. If he bids 2♠ raise to 4♠, otherwise continue with 3NT.
♠ A J 4 ♥ K 4 ♦ Q 9 7 6 ♣ J 7 5 4	2NT. 11-12 points but no 4-card major suit.

♠ A J 4 2 ♥ K 4 ♦ Q 9 7 6 ♣ J 10 5	2♣. Stayman. Bid an invitational 3♠ over 2♥, or 2NT over anything else.
♠ K 8 6 5 ♥ Q 10 6 4 ♦ J 8 6 5 4 ♣ –	2♣. Stayman. Pass any rebid, including 2♦.
♠ 4 ♥ K 8 6 5 ♦ Q 10 6 4 ♣ J 8 6 5	Pass. Don't use 2♣ Stayman because you are not prepared for a 2♠ rebid.
♠ A Q 2 ♥ A J 9 ♦ K Q 9 ♣ A Q 9 8	6NT. At least 34 points are present.

You open 1NT and your partner jumps to 3♠. What do you rebid with these hands?

♠ K 8 6 ♥ K 7 ♦ A J 7 6 ♣ Q 9 7 6	4♠. You have 3-card support so play in the 5-3 fit.
♠ K 8 ♥ K 7 4 ♦ A J 7 6 ♣ Q 9 7 6	3NT. Only doubleton support.

You open 1NT and your partner bids a Stayman 2♣. What is your rebid with these hands?

♠ K 7 6 4 ♥ K 7 6 4 ♦ A J ♣ Q 6 4	2♥. Show the lower major first. If partner continues with no trumps correct to spades.
♠ A J ♥ Q 6 4 ♦ K 7 6 4 ♣ K 7 6 4	2♦. Denies a 4-card major in response to Stayman.

Your partner opens 1NT and you make an enquiry about his major suit holdings by bidding a Stayman 2♣. His rebid is 2♥. How do you continue with these hands?

♠ K 8 5 4 ♥ A 10 8 ♦ K 8 ♣ J 10 9 7	2NT. 11-12 points. Denies four hearts and implies four spades.
♠ K 8 5 4 ♥ A 10 8 ♦ K 9 ♣ A 5 4 3	3NT. 13-19 points. Again you must have four spades.
♠ 9 ♥ 8 7 ♦ K 8 6 5 ♣ K J 10 6 5 4	3♣. A sign-off.
♠ A J 8 ♥ K 8 6 5 ♦ K 10 9 6 ♣ 7 5	3♥. Invitational. Partner will either raise to 4♥ with a maximum or he will pass with a minimum.

You open 1NT and in response to partner's Stayman 2♣ enquiry you rebid 2♥. He now jumps to 3NT. What should you do with these hands?

♠ A 6 4 ♥ K 7 5 4 ♦ Q J 6 2 ♣ K 8	Pass. Partner has four spades but you don't want to play in a 4-3 fit.
♠ Q J 6 2 ♥ K 7 5 4 ♦ A 6 4 ♣ K 8	4♠. Play in the 4-4 fit.

4 one of a suit opening bids

Life is easy if your partner opens 1NT. You know he is balanced with 12-14 points and you can easily guide the auction to a sensible conclusion. However, there is a cost. Because all hands of opening strength below 20 points are opened at the one level, it does mean that a wide variety of hands must be opened with one of a suit.

Since the opening bid is such a wide range of different hand types, how is responder to know what to do? The answer is that he cannot immediately take charge as he would after a 1NT opening bid. Instead he must start a discussion. The idea is that sooner or later one of the players will make a limit bid and then his partner will be able to take charge.

If you have sufficient values to open but are not suitable for 1NT, open one of your longest suit.

♠ A J 7 5
♥ K 8 6
♦ Q J 10
♣ A K J

This hand is balanced, but, with 19 points, it is too strong for an opening 1NT bid. Opener has to bid his longest suit. Open 1♠.

♠ J 9 7 5 4
♥ A K Q 3
♦ A 5
♣ A 2

Open 1♠. Your hearts are stronger, but it is quantity of trumps rather than quality that is vital. You can bid hearts next.

♠ K Q 5 4
♥ A 8
♦ K 7 6 4 3
♣ 7 6

Open 1♦, again it is not the suit with most high cards. You hope to bid spades next but over 2♣ you are not strong enough and will have to rebid 2♦.

With two suits of equal length, open the higher ranking.

♠ A Q 5 4 3	With both of these hands,	♠ A Q 7 5 2
♥ 8	open 1♠. You may have	♥ K 8
♦ A Q 5 4 3	the opportunity to bid your	♦ 8
♣ J 4	second suit later.	♣ K Q 4 3 2

♠ A 6 5	Open 1♥. You will bid no	♠ A 6 5
♥ A 7 4 3	trumps next so your minor	♥ A 7 4 2
♦ A Q 4 3	suit will probably never get	♦ K 8
♣ Q 8	a mention.	♣ A Q 7 4

It is vital to find a major suit fit if you have one, but with an 8-card minor suit fit, you normally prefer no trumps.

An exception to the rule. With two 4-card majors, open 1♥.

♠ A J 7 3	Open 1♥. The reason is that when you open
♥ A Q 6 4	the higher of two 4-card suits you sometimes
♦ 10 8	miss a fit in the lower one. This matters far
♣ A 7 5	more when the lower suit is a major. Partner
	will respond 1♠ with four or more spades.

Another exception is the hands with 4-4-4-1 shape.

These are the only unbalanced hands that do not contain a 5-card suit. The rules are:

♠ A Q 5 4	With a red suit singleton, open the suit below
♥ 2	the singleton. Open 1♦.
♦ A J 8 4	
♣ Q 4 3 2	

♠ 2	With a black suit singleton,	♠ A Q 5 4
♥ A Q 5 4	you will have three	♥ Q 4 3 2
♦ A J 8 4	touching suits – open the	♦ A J 8 4
♣ Q 4 3 2	middle of those suits.	♣ 2

With the hand on the left, open 1♦. With the hand on the right, open 1♥.

the rule of twenty

One way of judging whether a shapely hand is worth an opening is to add the high card points to the number of cards held in the two longest suits. If the total comes to at least 20 you can open. This is known as the RULE OF TWENTY.

♠ A J 9 8 6 5	This hand is very unbalanced with just 10
♥ A J 6 5 4	points. It is worth opening because of the
♦ 7	shape. With a major suit as trumps, the small
♣ 5	cards will take tricks. Using the rule of twenty
	this hand has 10 points, six spades and five
	hearts. 10 + 6 + 5 = 21. Open 1♠.

Before leaving the rule of twenty, a little clarification is necessary.

♠ A J 7 4 3	10 + 5 + 5 = 20 but the hand is not worth
♥ Q 8 7 5 4	opening. The singleton king is not worth
♦ K	3 points. Make it ♥ K Q 8 7 5 and a small
♣ 8 4	diamond and you would open 1♠.

Opener's rebids are discussed in detail in chapter 6 and it is not the intention to cover the ground here for unbalanced hands. However, we will look at balanced hands.

no trump rebids

If you open one of a suit and rebid in no trumps your rebid is a limit bid, which is not forcing. Responder can then take charge, using common sense, just as he would after a 1NT opening bid. A no trump rebid passes a very helpful message, namely the hand type is balanced and too strong for a 1NT opening bid.

VALUES NEEDED BY OPENER FOR NO TRUMP REBIDS		
	After 1♦ 1♠	After 1♦ 2♣
1NT	15-16 points	—
2NT	17-18 points	15-16 points
3NT	19 points	17-19 points

We can now look back to some earlier balanced hands which were only opened with one of a suit because they were too strong to open 1NT.

♠ A 6 5
♥ A 7 4 3
♦ A Q 4 3
♣ Q 8

You have 16 points. Open 1♥. Rebid 1NT if partner responds 1♠, or 2NT if the response is 2♣ or 2♦.

♠ A 6 5
♥ A 7 4 2
♦ K 8
♣ A Q 7 4

You have 17 points. Open 1♥. Rebid 2NT after a 1♠ response, or 3NT if responder bids 2♣ or 2♦.

♠ A J 7 3
♥ A Q 6 4
♦ 10 8
♣ A 7 5

You have 15 points. Open 1♥. If partner bids spades you will be delighted to support his suit. If he responds 2♣ or 2♦ your rebid will be 2NT.

We can also look again at hands with 5-3-3-2 shape. If the 5-card suit is a minor treat the hand as balanced, even if that means opening 1NT and never mentioning your suit. On the other hand a 5-card major should be bid. The hands below illustrate this principle.

♠ Q 7 5
♥ K 6
♦ K 8 4
♣ A J 7 5 4

Open 1NT with this 13 count.

♠ A 7 5
♥ K 8
♦ K 8 4
♣ A J 7 5 4

Open 1♣ and rebid 1NT with this 15 count if partner bids 1♦, 1♥ or 1♠.

♠ A J 7 5 4
♥ K 6
♦ K 8 4
♣ Q 7 5

Open 1♠. If partner responds 2♣, 2♦ or 2♥, rebid 2♠. You would like to rebid 2NT to show a balanced hand, but that promises 15-16 points. Your 2♠ rebid shows at least five spades.

♠ A J 7 5 4
♥ K 8
♦ K 8 4
♣ A 7 5

Open 1♠. This time you will be delighted to rebid 2NT if the response is 2♣, 2♦ or 2♥ as you have 15 points.

The fact that all no trump rebids show at least 15 points dictates your choice of opening bid.

♠ A K Q J
♥ K 8 3
♦ A 4 2
♣ 9 7 6

Open 1♠, planning to rebid in no trumps.

♠ A K Q J
♥ K 8 3
♦ 7 4 2
♣ 9 7 6

However, here you must open 1NT. What is your rebid over 2♣ if you open 1♠?

Say
'Thank you,
partner,' when
dummy goes
down

quiz on chapter 4

What is your opening bid with these hands? If you intend a no trump rebid after a response of 1♠ or 2♣, state what these rebids will be.

♠ K J 8 2 ♥ Q 10 8 2 ♦ A K 8 ♣ 10 4	Open 1NT. If you open with a suit bid you will have no rebid to show a balanced 13 points.
♠ K J 8 2 ♥ A 10 8 2 ♦ 10 8 ♣ A K 4	Open 1 ♥. Too strong for a 1NT opening. If partner bids spades you will support his suit. If partner responds 2♣ you will rebid 2NT, showing 15-16 points.
♠ K J 8 ♥ A 2 ♦ K 8 6 5 ♣ A Q 3 2	Open 1 ♦, the higher suit. Over 1♠ rebid 2NT, showing 17-18, over 2♣ rebid 3NT to show 17-19.
♠ A K 7 ♥ A J 10 8 ♦ K 8 ♣ A 6 5 4	Open 1 ♥ and rebid 3NT over 1♠ or 2♣.
♠ Q 3 ♥ A K 7 3 2 ♦ A 6 4 ♣ K 7 3	Open 1 ♥. Rebid 1NT after a response of 1♠ and 2NT over 2♣. These rebids shows 15-16 points.
♠ Q 3 ♥ K 7 3 ♦ 9 6 5 ♣ A K 7 3 2	Open 1NT to show a balanced 12-14 points. A 5-card minor suit shouldn't put you off this bid.
♠ K Q ♥ 2 ♦ A 10 5 4 3 ♣ J 9 7 5 4	Pass despite the rule of twenty! The ♠ K Q doubleton is not as useful as honour cards in your long suits.
♠ 8 4 ♥ 2 ♦ A 10 5 4 3 ♣ K Q J 4 3	Open 1 ♦, the higher 5-card suit. Open this hand because the honour cards are in the long suits.

♠ 2 ♥ J 9 7 3 2 ♦ K 7 ♣ A K Q J 7	Open 1♥ , the higher of two 5-card suits. The fact that your clubs are stronger is not relevant.
♠ J 6 ♥ A K Q 2 ♦ 9 2 ♣ A 7 4 3 2	Open 1♣, your longest suit.
♠ A J 8 7 ♥ K Q 10 3 ♦ 2 ♣ Q J 10 9	Open 1♣. With 4-4-4-1 shape and a red suit singleton open the suit below the singleton.
♠ 2 ♥ K Q 10 3 ♦ A J 8 7 ♣ Q J 10 9	Open 1♦ . With 4-4-4-1 shape and a black suit singleton open the middle of three touching suits.

What do you open with these hands? Although it is not covered till Chapter 6, see if you can guess your rebid when partner responds 1♠?

♠ 2 ♥ A K J 4 2 ♦ A Q J 5 3 ♣ 3 2	Open 1♥ . You will rebid 2♦ to show your second suit.
♠ Q 4 3 2 ♥ A K J 4 2 ♦ A 4 2 ♣ 5	Open 1♥ . You will rebid 2♠ to show 4-card support for spades.
♠ 2 ♥ K Q 10 3 ♦ A J 8 7 ♣ Q J 10 9	Open 1♦ . Rebid 2♣ over 1♠.
♠ A J 8 7 ♥ K Q 10 3 ♦ 2 ♣ Q J 10 9	Open 1♣. Raise your partner's spades by rebidding 2♠ which shows your 4-card spade support.

5 the first response

In any auction the sooner somebody makes a limit bid, the sooner his partner can take charge and determine the final contract. A principle of good bidding is that you try to investigate the suit at a low level by making forcing bids. When you know the suit, or no trumps, you make a limit bid.

In response to a one-level opening bid you pass if you have fewer than 6 points and find a bid with six or more points.

Why is this? Because partner could have as many as 19, so if you have 6 points a game contract might be possible. Don't worry too much about going down in a contract. If you play at the two level and go one down it is likely that your opponents could have made their own contract, and would have done so if you had passed. If the opening bid is one of a suit, the responses can be split into three distinct categories.

responder supports opener's major

If partner opens 1 ♥ or 1 ♠ it is your duty to support his suit if you have 4-card support. Your response is a limit bid, not forcing.

♠ K 8 4 3
♥ J 7 3 2
♦ A 7 4
♣ 8 7

In response to 1 ♥, 2 ♥ (a single raise) shows 6-9 points.

♠ K 8 4 3
♥ J 7 3 2
♦ A 7 4
♣ K 7

In response to 1 ♥, 3 ♥ (a double raise) shows 10-12 points.

♠ K 8 4 3
♥ J 7 3 2
♦ A 7 4
♣ A J

In response to 1♥, 4♥ (a triple raise) shows 13-15 points

♠ A J 7 4
♥ K J 5 4 3
♦ –
♣ 8 6 5 4

This hand is also worth raising 1♥ to 4♥, despite having only 9 points. The void diamond makes this hand worth a lot of tricks because you can trump the first diamond.

When supporting partner's suit a void in another suit is worth roughly the same as an ace. A singleton is worth about the same as a king and even a doubleton is an extra value. Appreciate shortage only after you have found a fit with partner.

After responder has made a limit raise, opener must use common sense to decide whether the final contract will be part-score, or game, (or even slam). Suppose you open 1♥ and your partner raises to 2♥. What should you do with these hands?

♠ 9 8
♥ A J 8 6 5
♦ K Q 6
♣ A 6 5

14 points and no great shape. 14 opposite 9 gives no realistic chance of game, so pass. Bidding on would be most misleading.

♠ 9 8
♥ A K J 6 5
♦ A K 6
♣ A 10 8

With 19 points you have a really good hand. Opposite 6-9 points you have at least 25, so you should be in game. Bid 4♥.

♠ 9
♥ A K J 6 5
♦ A K 9 4 2
♣ 8 3

With only 15 points, you might pass, but the shape is excellent. You have found a fit and your little hearts and diamonds should make tricks. Jump to 4♥.

♠ 9 8
♥ A K J 6 5
♦ A J 6
♣ A 9 8

You have 17 points. If responder has 8 or 9 points, there may be a game. You ask with an invitational raise to 3♥.

Partner need not worry that he has a bad hand, after all you know he has only 6-9 points by the raise to 2♥, so he can't have a good hand. He just decides whether it is good or bad for a 2♥ raise.

♠ J 7 2	1♥	2♥	♠ A 7 4 3
♥ Q 7 4 3	3♥	?	♥ 10 7 4 3
♦ Q 10 7			♦ 7 4
♣ J 6 3			♣ K J 2

simply pass with 6 points   …or bid 4♥ with 8 points

responder supports opener's minor

How about if partner opens with a minor suit? The point range for limit raises is the same, but there is one crucial difference. Finding an 8-card major suit fit tends to end the hunt for the correct denomination. You should give priority to introducing a major suit before supporting partner's minor. Suppose partner opens 1♣.

♠ 3 2
♥ K 8 2
♦ Q 10 8 7
♣ A J 8 6

You should jump to 3♣. This shows at least four clubs and 10-12 points. It is a limit bid.

♠ Q 10 8 7
♥ K 8 2
♦ 3 2
♣ A J 8 6

You should start with 1♠ in case opener has four spades and five clubs. Club support can come later.

responder bids a new suit

The message now is entirely different. If you raise partner's suit your message to him is "Good news, partner. We have a fit. I am bidding at the level I think we can make even if you are minimum." If you change suit you are still looking and want to keep the bidding low. Even if you have a powerful hand where you are confident game is making (13 or more points) it is still correct to show a new suit at the lowest possible level, leaving plenty of room to explore the best contract.

- To bid a new suit at the one level needs at least 6 points and a 4-card suit.

- To bid a new suit at the two level needs at least 9 points. The extra points compensate for raising the level. Normally a 4-card suit is sufficient but if partner opens 1♠ you require five hearts for a 2♥ response.

- To change suit with a jump is called a JUMP SHIFT. It says you have at least 16 points and a powerful suit with at least five cards. Game is definitely on, slam is possible.

♠ A J 7 4 ♥ 8 7 3 ♦ Q 5 2 ♣ 7 4 3	Partner opens 1♥. Bid 1♠ which shows at least four spades and at least 6 points. 1♠ is forcing, partner must make another bid. With this weak hand you expect to subside peacefully in a low level contract.
♠ A J 7 4 2 ♥ K 7 3 ♦ A Q 2 ♣ 7 4	Partner opens 1♥. Bid the same 1♠. It is forcing. Whatever partner bids, you will bid on to game even if partner's opening is weak.
♠ K 7 6 ♥ 7 6 ♦ 8 6 5 ♣ A Q 5 3 2	Respond to 1♥ with 2♣. 9 points and a 5-card suit is a minimum hand for the bid.

♠ 9 8
♥ K Q 3
♦ A 4
♣ A Q J 5 4 3

Jump to 3♣ over a 1♥ opening bid. This is forcing to game and promises at least 16 points.

which suit to respond?

When you have a choice of suits as responder the rules are:

- Plan your response to make sure a major suit fit will always be found. Only bypass bidding a 4-card major in favour of a longer minor if you have 12+ points.

- With the above constraint, bid your longest suit first.

- With two 5-card or 6-card suits bid the higher ranking first.

- With two 4-card suits bid the one that can be shown with the lowest level bid.

♠ A K 8 4
♥ 9
♦ A J 6 3 2
♣ 8 4 2

Respond to 1♣ with 1♦ and bid 2♦ over 1♥. With 12 points you are strong enough to bid diamonds first and spades next time. You would raise a 1♠ opening to 4♠.

♠ K 8 4 3 2
♥ 9
♦ A J 6 3 2
♣ 8 4

Respond to 1♣ or 1♥ with 1♠, the higher ranking of two 5-card suits. Even if partner opens 1♦ you should bid 1♠, looking for the major suit fit. If partner opens 1♠, bid 4♠.

♠ 7 4 3
♥ A Q 5 3
♦ A J 6 2
♣ 6 2

Bid 1♦ over 1♣ or 2♦ over 1♠, the lower ranking of two 4-card suits. This leaves room for partner to bid hearts, if he has four. You would raise a 1♥ opening to 3♥.

♠ A J 7 3
♥ 9 5
♦ 6 2
♣ Q 7 5 4 3

You don't have a choice of suits! You are not strong enough to respond at the two level, so you must respond 1♠ to 1♦ or 1♥ even though spades is not your longest suit.

responder bids no trumps

Almost all no trump bids are limit bids. That is because you usually convey the message of a balanced hand, which makes it easy for partner to know what to do.

In response to an opening one level bid any no trump response denies holding a major suit that could be bid at the one level. In response to 1♥ :

- 1NT shows 6-9 points.
- 2NT shows 10-12 points, balanced with no 5-card suit.
- 3NT shows 13-15 points, balanced with no 5-card suit.

You will notice that the word 'balanced' is missing from the description of the 1NT response. To see why, ask what your response to 1♠ would be with these hands.

♠ 6	You lack the 9 points	♠ 5 3
♥ A J 7 6	needed to bid a new suit at	♥ A J 7 6
♦ Q 5 3 2	the two level, but are too	♦ Q 7 6 4 3
♣ 7 5 4 3	good to pass.	♣ 7 2

The 1NT response is used as a 'dustbin' bid, for hands that merit a response but which have no suitable alternative available.

After a no trump response opener decides between part-score or game and between no trumps or a suit contract. Suppose you open 1♠ and partner jumps to 2NT.

♠ A J 7 5 4 2	2NT shows a balanced 10-12 points. Bid 3♠,
♥ Q J 5	a sign off. Your opening is weak, the values
♦ K 2	for game are not present, but partner must
♣ 8 6	have at least two spades.
♠ A J 7 5	Raise to 3NT. You have 15 points, partner has
♥ K 7 5	10-12. You must have at least 25 points
♦ A 8 6 5	between you.
♣ K 8	

quiz on chapter 5

For each of these hands, what is your response if partner opens:
(a) 1♣, (b) 1♦ , (c) 1♥ or (d) 1♠?

♠ 9 ♥ K 7 4 3 2 ♦ A 8 6 4 3 ♣ 7 4	(a) 1♥ . The higher of two 5-card suits. (b) 1♥ . Show your major suit first. (c) 3♥ . Shape makes up for only 7 points. (d) 1NT. Not enough points for 2♦ or 2♥ .
♠ K 8 4 3 ♥ 8 2 ♦ A 8 5 4 3 ♣ 8 5	(a) 1♦ . Your longest suit. (b) 1♠ . Show your major first. (c) 1♠ . Not strong enough for 2♦ . (d) 2♠ . 6-9 points and at least four spades.
♠ K Q 4 3 ♥ 8 2 ♦ A K 5 4 3 ♣ 8 5	(a) 1♦ . Your longest suit. (b) 1♠ . Show your major first. (c) 2♦ . Your longest suit. (d) 4♠ . 13-15 points (or equivalent shape)
♠ J 9 6 ♥ A 10 3 2 ♦ K 10 ♣ K 8 4 3	(a) 1♥ . Show your major first. (b) 1♥ . Bid a 4-card major before no trumps. (c) 3♥ . 10-12 points and at least four hearts. (d) 2NT. 10-12 points and a balanced hand.

You open 1♠. What do you bid if partner raises to:
(a) 2♠, (b) 3♠ or (c) 4♠?

♠ K Q 7 4 3 ♥ K 8 ♦ 9 4 2 ♣ A Q 3	(a) Pass. Not enough to invite game. (b) 4♠. Partner has 10-12 points. (c) Pass. Not enough for slam.

You open 1♠. What do you bid with these hands if partner responds
(a) 1NT, (b) 2NT or (c) 3NT?

♠ K J 7 3 ♥ A Q 2 ♦ 9 4 3 ♣ A K 7	(a) 2NT. Invites 3NT. (b) 3NT. (c) Pass.
♠ A K J 10 7 6 ♥ 2 ♦ K 7 4 ♣ Q 3 2	(a) 2♠. A sign off in the obvious contract. (b) 4♠. Worth game, and you have an 8-card spade fit. (c) 4♠.

6 opener rebids in a suit

In chapter 4 you saw how opener rebids no trumps with all balanced hands. Rebids in a suit after opener starts with a suit bid and responder changes suit can be grouped into three categories.

opener supports responder's suit

Because responder has shown at least a 4-card suit you will raise his suit if you have four or more. Raising partner's suit is a limit bid. You have found the correct denomination, so tell him about your strength.

If responder bids a new suit at the one level:

- A single raise (eg 1♣ – 1♠ – 2♠) shows 11-14 points.

- A double raise (eg 1♣ – 1♠ – 3♠) shows 15-17 points.

- A triple raise to game (eg 1♣ – 1♠ – 4♠) shows 18+ points.

♠ A J 7 3 ♥ K 8 ♦ Q 6 ♣ K 9 4 3 2	You open 1♣. You are pleasantly surprised when partner responds 1♠. You must immediately show your support. Rebid 2♠.
♠ A J 7 3 ♥ K 8 ♦ A Q ♣ K 9 4 3 2	You open 1♣ and partner bids 1♠. Show your support and strength by bidding 3♠. Responder now knows you have five or more clubs, at least four spades and 15-17 points. Common sense should allow him to select the correct contract.

♠ 8
♥ A J 7 3
♦ A 6
♣ A 10 9 4 3 2

You open 1♣ and partner bids 1♥. This hand doesn't have enough points for 3♥, but it has excellent shape. Remember, when supporting partner a singleton is worth roughly as much as a king. Bid 3♥ and hope partner goes 4♥.

If responder bids a new suit at the two level:

■ A single raise (eg 1♥ – 2♣ – 3♣) shows 11-15 points.

■ A double raise (eg 1♥ – 2♣ – 4♣) shows 16+ points.

If the bidding starts 1♠ – 2♥ then responder has shown five hearts, so opener can and should raise hearts whenever he has 3-card support.

♠ A J 7 3 2
♥ K 7 3
♦ 9
♣ K J 5 3

You open 1♠.
If partner responds 2♣ you raise to 3♣.
If partner responds 2♥ you raise to 3♥.

♠ A K J 3 2
♥ K 7 3
♦ 9
♣ A J 3 2

You open 1♠.
If partner responds 2♣ you raise to 4♣.
If partner responds 2♥ you raise to 4♥.

Raising partner's suit to show support takes a very high priority in the bidding.

Just about the only time you don't show your support is if his response was in a minor suit and you are intending a no trump rebid. Yet again, minor suits are brushed aside in order to find the no trump contract.

♠ A K J 8
♥ K 7 3
♦ K 2
♣ K J 8 7

You open 1♠ and partner bids 2♣. Jump to 3NT. Don't support clubs.

opener rebids his own suit

If opener repeats his own suit without responder having supported it, he shows extra length. The higher the rebid, the stronger the suit must be. This is because, although it may be quite likely that responder has something (if only a doubleton) in the suit, it is equally possible there is void opposite.

If opener decides to rebid his suit after responder changes suit, it is a limit bid:

- A simple rebid (eg 1♥ – 1♠ – 2♥) shows 11-14 points and at least five hearts.

- A jump rebid (eg 1♥ – 1♠ – 3♥) shows 15-17 points and at least six good hearts.

- A double jump rebid (eg 1♥ – 1♠ – 4♥) shows 16 or more points and at least seven good hearts.

♠ 10 4 ♥ A 10 9 7 5 ♦ A K 6 ♣ Q J 7	You open 1♥ and partner responds 1♠. What now? Rebid 2♥. Although balanced this hand is too weak for a 15-16 point 1NT rebid.
♠ 10 8 ♥ A Q J 6 5 4 ♦ A Q 8 ♣ K 7	You open 1♥ and partner responds 1♠. Rebid 3♥.
♠ 10 4 ♥ A 10 9 6 5 ♦ A K 6 ♣ A J 6	You open 1♥ and partner responds 1♠. Rebid 1NT showing 15-16 points.
♠ K 8 ♥ J 8 7 4 3 2 ♦ A K ♣ A Q 4	Rebid 2NT. You must improvise here. The hand is too strong for 2♥ and the suit is too weak for 3♥. The least misleading bid is 2NT, showing a balanced 17-18 points.

opener bids a third suit

Often, by the time opener has made his rebid one of the partners has made a limit bid. This happens when:

- Somebody bids no trumps.
- Somebody supports his partner's suit.
- Somebody rebids his own suit.

How about if opener introduces a third suit? To understand the message given, you need to mentally construct a barrier exactly one level above the opening bid. Thus, if the opening bid was 1♦, the barrier is 2♦. Think of it as a safety barrier.

You	Partner
1♦	2♣
2♠	

3♦
3♣
2NT
2♠
2♥
■■■■
2♦
2♣
1NT
1♠
1♥
1♦

If you rebid a new suit above this barrier, you show at least 16 points and guarantee at least five cards in your first suit. Bidding a new suit above the barrier is called a REVERSE. For example, in this auction you show you have longer diamonds than spades because with equal length you would have opened the higher suit.

You	Partner
1♦	1♠
2♣	

If you rebid a new suit below this barrier, you show no extra strength and responder can pass. You usually have at least five cards in the first suit. This is because you are passing the message of an unbalanced hand by your failure to open or rebid no trumps. The only unbalanced hand without a 5-card suit is the 4-4-4-1 shape.

You	Partner	In this auction you might have five hearts and
1♥	2♦	only four clubs, or you might have five of each
3♣		or even six of each. This auction is forcing to

game because you need 16+ to reverse and partner has shown 9+ with his two-level bid.

You	Partner	If you bid a new suit with a jump, you show at
1♥	1♠	least 19 points or the equivalent in a shapely
3♣		hand. This auction is forcing to game because

your 19 is facing at least 6 points.

What choices do you have, after the auction

Partner	You	Partner shows a minimum unbalanced hand
1♥	1♠	with at least five hearts and at least four
2♦		diamonds.

♠ K J 6 4 3
♥ 2
♦ J 7 4
♣ J 8 4 3

You can pass 2♦ when you are weak and prefer diamonds to hearts, leaving South to play 2♦.

♠ K J 8 7
♥ 9 7 5
♦ 7 4 3
♣ Q 5 4

You know partner should have five hearts so bid 2♥. When your partner bids two suits and you are weak, you often end up deciding between his suits, not because you like either but simply to end the auction quickly.

To revert to partner's first suit is called PREFERENCE. Don't mistake preference for real support.

You	Partner	To understand why a reverse shows extra
1♥	2♦	strength and is forcing, look at this auction. If
3♣		partner wants to give preference to hearts, the

lowest legal heart bid is 3♥. The auction uses up more space, hence the need for extra strength.

♠ 7 4	You open 1♥. Partner responds with 2♣.
♥ K Q 10 6 5	Rebid 2♦, showing about 12-16 points, at least
♦ K 7 3 2	four diamonds and normally at least five hearts.
♣ A 7	If partner gives preference to 2♥ you will pass.

♠ A 4	You open 1♥. Partner responds with 2♣.
♥ K Q 10 6 5	Despite 16 points it is not strong enough for a
♦ K 7 3 2	jump to 3♦. Rebid 2♦, even though you are an
♣ A 7	ace stronger than the hand before. If partner
	bids 2♥, invite with 3♥, showing extra values.

♠ K J 3 2	You open 1♥. Partner responds with 2♣. A
♥ K Q 10 6 5	rebid of 2♠ would be above the barrier of 2♥.
♦ 7 4	You are not strong enough to reverse into 2♠
♣ A 7	so you must rebid 2♥.

♠ K J 3 2	You open 1♥. Partner responds with 2♣. Now
♥ K Q 10 6 5	you are strong enough to reverse into 2♠,
♦ A 4	showing at least 16 points, five or more hearts
♣ A 7	and four spades. This is game forcing,
	because partner has shown at least 9 points
	with his 2♣ response.

You open 1♥. What should you rebid over 1♠? Over 2♦?

♠ 5	Over 1♠ you are delighted to show your
♥ K Q 10 6 5	second suit with 2♣.
♦ Q 10	Over 2♦ you are not strong enough for a
♣ A J 8 7 3	reverse into 3♣. Rebid 2♥. Your club suit
	may be lost.

♠ 5	Over 1♠ you bid 2♣. You hope to have
♥ K Q 10 6 5	another chance to show your extra strength.
♦ A K	Over 2♦ you have the extra strength to
♣ A J 8 7 3	reverse into 3♣, which is game forcing.

quiz on chapter 6

With each of the following hands you open 1♦. What is your rebid if partner responds 1♠?

♠ 7 5 ♥ A K ♦ K Q 10 9 4 2 ♣ A 10 7	3♦. 15-17 points and at least six good diamonds.
♠ 7 5 ♥ K 2 ♦ K Q 10 9 4 2 ♣ A 10 7	2♦. 11-14 points and at least five diamonds.
♠ K J 8 4 ♥ A 5 ♦ A Q 4 3 2 ♣ Q 3	3♠. 15-17 points and at least 4-card spade support.
♠ K J 8 4 ♥ J 5 ♦ A Q 4 3 2 ♣ Q 3	2♠. 11-14 points and at least 4-card spade support.
♠ 7 5 ♥ A Q 2 ♦ K J 10 6 3 ♣ K 6 3	2♦. You should have opened 1NT.
♠ 7 5 ♥ A Q 2 ♦ A Q 10 6 3 ♣ K 6 3	1NT. 15-16 points and balanced.
♠ 5 ♥ A K 10 2 ♦ K J 10 6 3 ♣ Q 9 2	2♦. Too weak for a 2♥ reverse.
♠ 5 ♥ A K 10 2 ♦ K J 10 6 3 ♣ A Q 2	2♥. A reverse. At least 17 points with longer diamonds than hearts. A forcing bid.

♠ 6 ♥ Q 9 2 ♦ K J 10 6 3 ♣ A K 10 2	2♣. Showing at least five diamonds and four clubs but quite a wide strength range.
♠ 6 ♥ A Q 2 ♦ K J 10 6 3 ♣ A K 10 2	2♣. Top of the range but not worth a game forcing 3♣. 2NT is possible, showing 17-18 points, but a singleton is not normal for a no trump bid.
♠ 6 ♥ A Q 2 ♦ A Q 4 3 2 ♣ A K 10 2	3♣. 19+ points and game forcing,
♠ 6 ♥ A K 10 2 ♦ A Q 4 3 2 ♣ A Q 2	2♥. A reverse. This is forcing, you intend to listen to partner and bid game next time.

Your partner opens 1♥ and rebids 2♠ after your 1♠ response. How do you continue with these hands?

♠ K Q 6 5 3 ♥ 8 4 3 ♦ K 10 3 ♣ 9 7	Pass. No prospect of game opposite 11-14 points.
♠ K Q 6 5 3 ♥ 8 4 3 ♦ A K 3 ♣ J 7	4♠. Plenty for game.
♠ K Q 6 5 3 ♥ 8 4 3 ♦ A J 3 ♣ J 7	3♠. Invites partner to bid 4♠ if maximum.
♠ K Q 10 8 5 4 ♥ 10 4 ♦ A 9 7 6 4 ♣ —	4♠. The distribution more than compensates for the shortage of points.

You open 1♥ and raise your partner's 1♠ response to 2♠. He continues with 3♠. What should you do with these hands?

♠ K Q 5 4 ♥ A J 7 5 4 ♦ Q 10 ♣ 10 9	Pass. You are minimum.
♠ K Q 5 4 ♥ A J 7 5 4 ♦ A 10 ♣ 10 9	4♠. You have a maximum 2♠ raise.

You respond to your partner's 1♥ opening bid with 1♠. How should you continue with these hands if he rebids 2♥?

♠ A 8 6 5 4 ♥ K 9 2 ♦ 4 3 ♣ K 7 2	3♥. Invitational to 4♥.
♠ A 8 6 5 4 ♥ K 9 2 ♦ 4 3 ♣ A Q 2	4♥. Well worth game.
♠ Q 9 6 5 4 ♥ 10 ♦ K 9 5 ♣ Q 10 8 7	Pass. Any attempt by you to improve the contract will only make matters worse.
♠ A Q 5 4 ♥ 10 ♦ A 9 6 2 ♣ J 10 7 5	2NT. 10-12 points. Invitational to game.

7 responder's second bid

We have already seen how responder uses common sense when opener's rebid is a limit bid. In this chapter we see how responder decides what to do when opener bids a third suit without a reverse or jump. The options open to responder depend on whether he is:

- weak (6-9 points)

- intermediate (10-12 points)

- strong (13+ points)

These numbers are not hard to remember. They are the same as the immediate responses to a 1♥ opening bid when you bid no trumps or support opener's suit.

responder is weak (6-9 points)

Suppose the auction starts

Opener	Responder
1♦	1♠
2♣	?

Responder has three options.

♠ K J 7 4 3　　　Firstly, **he can pass** because he prefers
♥ K 7　　　　　opener's second suit.
♦ 8 4
♣ 8 6 5 4

♠ K 10 7 5 4	Or **he can give preference** to opener's first
♥ 8 7	suit, by bidding 2♦. He prefers diamonds
♦ Q 3 2	because South might have longer diamonds
♣ Q 3 2	than clubs but certainly won't have longer
	clubs than diamonds.

♠ K 10 7 5 4	Here too, it is best to **give preference** to 2♦.
♥ 9 8 4 3	South probably has five diamonds, this hand
♦ J 7	demonstrates that preference is not the same
♣ Q 7	as enthusiasm!

♠ A Q J 7 5 4	**He can repeat his own suit** by bidding 2♠,
♥ 9 8 4	showing at least six spades. The spade suit in
♦ 7 5	the previous hand isn't good enough to repeat
♣ 7 5	the spades with 2♠.

responder has intermediate strength (10-12 points)

Consider responder's options after the same auction with a slightly stronger hand.

Opener	Responder
1♦	1♠
2♣	?

♠ K 8 6 5 4	**He can make a jump preference bid,** to give
♥ 6 4	real preference to opener's first suit. In the
♦ K J 5	auction given, jump to 3♦, which guarantees
♣ A 10 2	at least 3-card support.

♠ A J 7 5 4	**He can raise opener's second suit** with
♥ 9 5	4-card or longer support. This hand raises to
♦ Q 2	3♣.
♣ K 8 7 5	

♠ K Q 10 9 4 3	**He can repeat his own suit with a jump bid.**
♥ 6 4	This shows at least a strong 6-card suit. With
♦ A 7	this hand jump to 3♠.
♣ J 5 3	

♠ A 10 7 4 2	**He can bid 2NT** with a stopper in the unbid
♥ A J 8	suit. ♥ A J 8 is a good enough holding to bid
♦ Q 4	2NT on this 11 count.
♣ 10 5 3	

Logic dictates that none of these bids is forcing because they limit the hand. Opener will move on to game unless he is minimum.

But what if responder cannot support either of opener's suits, doesn't have a strong 6-card spade suit and doesn't have a heart stopper? It is worth commenting that while it is perfectly reasonable to bid no trumps early in the auction with a relatively weak suit, now that you have told the enemy to lead hearts you must be prepared! The answer is to bid 2♥, the fourth suit. More of that in a minute!

responder is strong enough for game (13 or more points)

Holding 13 or more points, it is the duty of responder to make sure game is reached. Using the same auction as before.

Opener	Responder
1♦	1♠
2♣	?

♠ A 9 7 3	**Responder can bid game in either of**
♥ 2	**Opener's suits or his own suit.** With good
♦ K 8 7 4 3	diamonds, he gives strong preference with
♣ A J 6	5♦.

♠ A 8 7 5 4   With good clubs, it is simple and sensible to
♥ 3   raise to game. Note that the excellent shape
♦ K 8   of these two hands makes up for a slight
♣ A J 6 4 2   deficiency in points.

♠ K Q J 9 8 6 4   With good spades, its best to jump to game by
♥ 9 7   bidding 4♠. Since opener may be void in
♦ 7   spades responder needs at least seven strong
♣ A K 2   spades.

♠ A K 8 6
♥ A Q 6   Alternatively, with a stopper in the fourth suit
♦ 9 8 3   responder can bid 3NT.
♣ J 8 3

If he cannot think of anything else to bid, then 2♥, the fourth suit,
may come to his rescue.

the fourth suit

This is an advanced topic. If you are in your first year of learning
you would do well to give it a miss.

	Opener	Responder
♠ A Q 8 6 2		
♥ 8 7 5	1♦	1♠
♦ Q 7	2♣	?
♣ A 10 9		

What can responder bid now?

■ the spades are not good enough to jump to 3♠.

■ he cannot raise either minor suit.

■ he doesn't have a heart stopper for no trumps.

He bids 2♥, the fourth suit, a conventional bid asking opener to
describe his hand further. The fourth suit hardly has a natural use

because if responder had both major suits and reasonable values he would bid no trumps. To use the fourth suit you need at least intermediate values. Opener may have any of these hands:

♠ 7
♥ A J 9
♦ K J 8 6 5
♣ K 8 7 6

With this hand, he rebids 2NT showing a minimum with a heart stopper.

♠ 7
♥ A J 9
♦ A K 10 9 2
♣ K 8 7 6

Here he jumps to 3NT which shows extra points and a heart stopper.

♠ J 4 3
♥ 2
♦ A J 8 6 5
♣ K Q J 2

With 3-card support for spades in a minimum hand he bids 2♠.

♠ K 4 3
♥ 2
♦ A K 10 9 2
♣ K Q 8 2

This hand is suitable for 3♠, showing three spades and extra points.

♠ 7
♥ 6 4
♦ A K J 3 2
♣ K Q 7 4 3

Here he shows his fifth club with 3♣. This bid does not show any extra strength.

♠ 7
♥ 6 4
♦ A K 8 5 3 2
♣ K Q 4 3

With a sixth diamond he rebids 3♦, suggesting six diamonds and four clubs. Like a club rebid, 3♦ does not show extra strength.

There is only one auction where the fourth suit can be bid at the one level and then it is used as a natural (but still forcing) bid, as illustrated on this hand:

West	East	West	East
♠ K J 7 4	♠ Q 10 6 2	1♣	1♦
♥ A 7 4 2	♥ 8	1♥	1♠
♦ 8	♦ A J 6 3 2	3♠	4♠
♣ A K 3 2	♣ Q J 5		

If East had wanted to make a fourth-suit enquiry bid he would have had to jump to 2♠.

Fourth-suit forcing at the two level may be only intermediate strength. In the next example West shows his minimum opening bid with a diamond stopper with 2NT. If East had intermediate strength he could pass 2NT, but having game values he raises to 3NT.

West	East	West	East
♠ 6 2	♠ A K 5 4 3	1♥	1♠
♥ K Q J 5 3	♥ 10 2	2♣	2♦
♦ A Q	♦ 9 4 2	2NT	3NT
♣ J 8 3 2	♣ A Q 4		

Fourth-suit forcing at the three level gives less room for manoeuvre so it is sensible to play it as game forcing. In the next hand East doesn't have an easy bid after 2♥. He decides to make the slight overbid of 3♣, the fourth suit, even though it commits his side to game.

West	East	West	East
♠ A 8 7 3 2	♠ Q 4	1♠	2♦
♥ K Q 5 4 2	♥ A 10 8	2♥	3♣
♦ K 7	♦ A Q 9 3 2	3♥	4♥
♣ 6	♣ 9 7 2		

quiz on chapter 7

State North's second bid after the auction:

South	North
1♠	2♣
2♦	?

♠ 8 ♥ A J 6 5 ♦ K 7 2 ♣ A Q 9 3 2	3NT. You have no fit with partner, but game values and a good heart stopper.
♠ 8 4 ♥ 7 4 3 ♦ K 7 2 ♣ A K J 5 3	2♥, the fourth suit. You have intermediate values with no obvious bid to make.

What should be North's second bid after the auction:

South	North
1♠	2♣
2♥	?

♠ 8 ♥ A J 6 5 ♦ K 7 2 ♣ A Q 9 3 2	4♥. An excellent fit and game values. If anything, you are too strong for this bid, but the important thing is to find a sensible contract.
♠ 8 4 ♥ 7 4 3 ♦ K 7 2 ♣ A K J 5 3	2NT. 10-12 points with a stopper in diamonds, the fourth suit.

What should be North's second bid after the auction:

South	North
1♦	2♣
2♠	?

♠ 8 ♥ A J 6 5 ♦ K 7 2 ♣ A Q 9 3 2	3NT is a common sense bid. Again, you will be much more concerned with missing a slam than failing in 3NT. Remember, partner has shown at least 16 points for his reverse.
♠ 8 4 ♥ 7 4 3 ♦ K 7 2 ♣ A K J 5 3	3♥, the fourth suit. You have plenty for game because partner has reversed.

What should South's third bid be with these hands after the auction:

South	North
1♥	1♠
2♣	2♦
?	

♠ J 8 7 ♥ A J 10 3 2 ♦ J ♣ A K Q 6	2♦ is the fourth suit. It asks partner for more information. Jump to 3♠ to show your 3-card spade support in a hand which isn't minimum.
♠ 6 ♥ A J 9 5 4 3 ♦ 5 4 ♣ A Q 7 2	Bid 2♥ to show a minimum opening bid with an extra heart. You usually have five hearts to open 1♥ and rebid 2♣, so this suggests a sixth heart.
♠ 6 ♥ A J 10 3 2 ♦ K Q 10 ♣ A J 7 2	Jump to 3NT. You have the diamonds well stopped and you are not minimum.
♠ 6 2 ♥ A Q 6 3 2 ♦ J ♣ K Q 9 5 3	Bid 3♣ to show you have five clubs. This confirms you have five hearts too because you always bid your longest suit first.
♠ 7 ♥ A K 7 4 3 2 ♦ 6 ♣ A Q J 4 3	Jump to 4♣. You have an excellent hand and want to play a game contract in one of your suits.
♠ 2 ♥ A 8 7 5 4 ♦ Q 10 8 ♣ A Q 3 2	Bid 2NT, showing a minimum opening bid. You just have to hope your diamond holding provides a stopper.

8 opening bids at the two level

So far we have considered hands with up to 20 points. The danger with opening stronger hands than this with a one-level bid is that partner may pass and you will miss a good game contract. If your number of points starts with a two it is usually best to announce the good news by opening at the two level.

Strong hands are opened with two-level bids. The extra strength justifies opening at the higher level.

the 2NT opening bid

An opening 2NT shows a balanced hand with 20-22 points. The responses are similar to those to 1NT, except you are unable to sign off at the three level.

In response to 2NT:

- 3♣ is Stayman, asking for a 4-card major.

- 3♥ and 3♠ show 5-card suits, asking opener to raise with 3-card or better support or to rebid 3NT with just doubleton support. You require 4 or more points for this.

- 3NT is a sign-off bid, requiring 4-10 points.

- 4♥ and 4♠ are sign-off bids, showing four or more points and at least a 6-card suit.

- 4NT invites 6NT and shows 11-12 points.

♠ Q 10 7 4 ♥ 8 4 ♦ 8 5 3 2 ♣ K J 3	You have 6 points, enough to bid game. Bid 3♣ which is Stayman. Now you will find out if partner has a 4-card spade suit. Bid 3NT over partner's response of 3♦ or 3♥. Raise 3♠ to 4♠.
♠ K J 7 4 3 ♥ 8 4 ♦ 8 3 2 ♣ J 8 6	You have 5 points, enough to bid game. Bid 3♠. Partner will bid 3NT with just two spades but 4♠ with three or more.
♠ K J 7 4 3 2 ♥ 8 4 ♦ 8 3 2 ♣ J 6	With a 6-card suit you want to play in spades. Bid 4♠. Remember partner shows at least two spades with the opening 2NT bid.
♠ 8 3 2 ♥ 8 4 ♦ K J 7 4 3 ♣ J 8 6	Don't introduce diamonds, just raise to 3NT. Bid minor suits with more caution. 3♦ would show at least 7 points. It is forcing and often looking for a slam.

the conventional 2♣ opening bid

You have now seen how to deal with balanced hands of up to 22 points. Sometimes the gods of fortune are even kinder to you and you are dealt an even stronger, balanced hand. You then have to use a 2♣ opening bid which is conventional and unconditionally forcing.

The 2♣ opening bid shows 23 or more points, maybe slightly fewer if the playing strength is so good that game should be attempted opposite nothing. With one exception, the 2♣ opening is forcing to game.

If your partner opens 2♣ and you have fewer than 8 points you respond with a conventional 2♦, called the NEGATIVE response. All other responses are POSITIVE, forcing to game and showing an ace and a king or any hand with 8+ points. Of course most of the time the response to 2♣ is 2♦. If you give a positive response to 2♣, a slam will often be reached.

The 2♣ opening bid doesn't initially show a balanced hand, only when it is followed by a no trump rebid. The 2♣ opening bid is a conventional catch-all bid for all very strong hands that are worth forcing to game.

♠ A Q 7 4
♥ K 7
♦ A K 5 4
♣ A K 10

Open 2♣ and rebid 2NT over 2♦. This shows a balanced hand with 23-24 points, and is the one and only sequence after an opening 2♣ bid that is not unconditionally forcing to game. With nothing, partner can pass. Bidding over 2NT is like bidding over a 2NT opening, but every bid requires two fewer points.

♠ A K Q 4
♥ K 7
♦ A K 5 4
♣ A K 10

Open 2♣ and rebid 3NT over 2♦, showing a balanced hand with 25-28 points.

♠ A Q J 7 5
♥ A K 4 2
♦ A Q J
♣ A

Open 2♣ and rebid 2♠ over 2♦. This is game forcing, and will give you time subsequently to show your hearts. If responder really does have rubbish he has a conventional second negative bid available in 2NT over 2♥ or 2♠.

♠ A K J 6
♥ 9
♦ A K Q 2
♣ A K 3 2

Open 2♣ and rebid 2♠ over 2♦. You would prefer a 5-card suit, but you have no real alternative.

A 2NT response to a 2♣ opening bid is natural, showing a balanced hand with 8 or more points.

♠ 7 5	Respond to 2♣ with 2NT. To respond 2♥ you
♥ J 8 7 6 2	require better hearts than this. It is not wise to
♦ A K 7	introduce a poor quality suit if it is likely that
♣ 10 9 4	the auction will end up at slam level.

♠ 4 3	Jump to 3♥ over 2♣. This shows a solid suit
♥ A K Q 10 6 4 3	of at least six cards and instructs partner that
♦ 6	hearts will be trumps.
♣ 9 5 2	

strong two-bids

The strong two-bids are: 2♦, 2♥ and 2♠. They often feature hands in the 20-22 point range but, when deciding whether to open with one of these bids, look less at the number of points and more at the playing strength.

To open a strong two-bid you need a good suit (at least five cards) and a hand where you would expect to take at least eight tricks with no help from partner. This is often called 'having at least eight playing tricks'. There isn't a bid to show eight playing tricks in clubs because we use the 2♣ opening as conventional for very strong hands.

A 5-card suit should be no weaker than A Q J 6 5.

A 6-card suit should be no weaker than A J 9 6 5 4.

So how do we calculate our playing tricks? Playing tricks are the number of tricks you would expect to take if partner has been dealt a balanced hand with no points at all. You assume reasonable breaks.

For example:

♠ A Q J 8 7 6   is five tricks. You expect to lose a trick to the ♠K but no other trick.

♠ K Q 10 9 7 6 is four tricks. You will probably lose to the ♠A and ♠J.

♠ Q J 9 6 5 4 is about three tricks. You will lose the ♠A and ♠K, and more often than not to the ♠10.

Note that your estimates are somewhat pessimistic because you are assuming you cannot reach dummy to take vital finesses. If partner produces one trick that will often be sufficient opposite your eight trick hand to make ten tricks because it is also an entry card.

Responder has a conventional negative response of 2NT to show a hand with fewer than 8 points (although an ace and a king are worth a positive response). Aces and kings tend to be particularly useful opposite a strong two-bid because such bids tend to be distributional, showing length in one or two suits and corresponding shortage elsewhere. Similarly, queens and jacks are often useless unless they are in opener's suit (or suits).

♠ A Q J 8 6 5　Strong two-bids can be one-suited hands.
♥ A K　　　　　This has eight tricks: five spades, two hearts
♦ 8 3　　　　　and the ♣A. Open 2♠.
♣ A J 2

♠ A Q J 8 6 2　Strong two-bids can also be two-suited hands.
♥ A K J 3 2　　This hand has nine tricks: five spades and
♦ K 7　　　　　four hearts. Open 2♠.
♣ −

A strong two-bid is forcing for one round to allow opener to show a second suit.

To see why consider this hand opposite the last one.

♠ 7　　　　　　Obviously you would pass 2♠ if you could and
♥ 7 6 5 4　　　an excellent 4♥ contract would be missed.
♦ 10 8 5 4　　　Respond 2NT, a negative bid, to a 2♠ opener.
♣ 8 7 6 3　　　Raise the 3♥ rebid to 4♥.

♠ K 7 3	Respond to 2♠ with 2NT to show fewer than
♥ 8 4 2	8 points. You will make sure that the bidding
♦ K 7 6 4	reaches a game contract by bidding 4♠ on
♣ 8 5 2	the next round.

Here are examples of auctions that can terminate at the three-level after a strong two-bid.

South	North	South rebids his suit at the lowest level. North
2♠	2NT	can pass with a dreadful hand.
3♠		

South	North	South rebids his second suit, which is a
2♠	2NT	forcing bid, but North gives simple preference
3♦	3♠	to spades. If North had anything useful he
		would bid 4♠.

We now turn to a happier scenario, when you have a positive response to a 2♠ opening bid. Simply bid your hand naturally.

♠ 7 3	Respond 3NT. This shows a balanced hand
♥ Q 6 4	with 8-11 points.
♦ K J 5 3	
♣ K 10 4 3	

♠ 8 3	Bid 3♦, showing a good 5-card suit.
♥ 9 6 3	
♦ A Q 6 4 3	
♣ K 10 2	

♠ K 7 3	Raise to 3♠. 3-card support for spades is
♥ 7 3	ample, but you need at least one ace for the
♦ A Q 10 8	single raise. This helps partner judge whether
♣ 10 6 5 3	a slam may be possible.

♠ K 7 3	Jump to 4♠. This denies an ace and shows
♥ Q 10 7 2	less useful cards. Remember, aces and kings
♦ Q 8 4	are always useful, queens and jacks in the
♣ Q 6 4	side suits less so.

quiz on chapter 8

What do you open with these hands? If you open with a strong two-bid what is your rebid after the 2NT negative response? If you open 2♣ what is your rebid after a 2♦ negative response?

♠ A Q 7 ♥ A J 7 ♦ A Q 10 4 ♣ K J 9	2NT. Balanced 20-22 points.
♠ A Q 7 ♥ A K 7 ♦ A Q 10 4 ♣ K J 9	2♣. Rebid 2NT after 2♦ to show 23-24 balanced points.
♠ A Q 7 ♥ A K 7 ♦ A K J 4 ♣ K J 9	2♣. Rebid 3NT after 2♦ to show 25-28 balanced points.
♠ A 8 5 4 3 ♥ A Q ♦ A K 9 ♣ K J 9	2NT. The spades are not strong enough for 2♠.
♠ A Q ♥ A Q 4 2 ♦ A K ♣ A K J 8 6	2♣. Rebid 3♣ after 2♦, game forcing.
♠ A K Q 10 6 5 ♥ 7 ♦ A 7 2 ♣ A J 7	2♠. Rebid 3♠ after 2NT, not forcing.
♠ A Q J 7 6 5 ♥ A 5 ♦ A J 10 7 6 ♣ −	2♠. Rebid 3♦ after 2NT. This is forcing but if responder gives preference to 3♠ it can be passed.
♠ K 8 7 5 4 ♥ − ♦ A K 8 6 5 ♣ A K Q	1♠. The spades are too poor for 2♠ and the hand is not strong enough for 2♣.

What do you respond to 2NT with these hands?

♠ 6 5 ♥ K Q 8 7 ♦ 6 5 2 ♣ 10 9 7 4	3♣. Stayman. Play in 4♥ if a 4-4 fit is found, otherwise settle for 3NT.
♠ 6 5 ♥ K Q 5 3 2 ♦ 6 5 2 ♣ 10 8 4	3♥. Opener will raise to 4♥ with 3-card or better support and will rebid 3NT otherwise.
♠ 6 5 ♥ 6 5 2 ♦ K Q 5 3 2 ♣ 10 8 4	3NT. Nine tricks are easier than eleven.
♠ 6 5 ♥ K Q 9 5 3 2 ♦ 6 5 2 ♣ 10 8	4♥. A sign-off.

Your partner opens 2♣. What do you respond with these hands?

♠ J 8 7 4 2 ♥ K 10 5 2 ♦ Q 9 8 ♣ 7	2♦. The negative response denying 8 points.
♠ J 8 ♥ K 10 5 2 ♦ A Q 4 3 ♣ 10 8 4	2NT, showing 8+ points with no good suit.
♠ A K Q J 7 4 ♥ 8 7 ♦ 10 9 6 ♣ 8 6	3♠. A solid suit of at least six cards.
♠ 7 5 4 3 2 ♥ K 8 ♦ K J 7 ♣ Q 5 2	2NT. Forget the spades. The suit is far too weak in a hand that is likely to end in a slam.

Your partner opens with a strong 2♠ bid. What do you respond with these hands?

♠ K 9 7 4 ♥ 7 3 ♦ 8 6 4 ♣ J 8 6 5	2NT. You intend to play in 4♠, but you first give the negative response which denies 8 points.
♠ K 9 2 ♥ 8 7 ♦ A 6 4 3 ♣ J 10 7 4	3♠. A positive that included an ace. Game forcing, of course.
♠ K 9 2 ♥ 8 7 ♦ K 8 6 5 ♣ Q 10 7 4	4♠. A positive without an ace.

With the hands below you open 2NT. What is your second bid if your partner responds: (a) 3♣ (b) 3♦ (c) 3♥? (d) 3♠?

♠ K Q 3 2 ♥ A 8 6 3 ♦ A J 10 ♣ A Q	(a) 3♥. Your cheaper 4-card major. (b) 4♦ (c) 4♥ (d) 4♠
♠ K 10 ♥ K 8 7 ♦ K Q 10 7 ♣ A K Q J	(a) 3♦. Denying a 4-card major. (b) 4♦. Good support. (c) 4♥. Partner has five hearts. (d) 3NT, showing a doubleton spade.

What do you open with?

♠ Q 8 7 5 4 ♥ A K Q 3 ♦ A ♣ A Q 4	Some hands are very strong, but are neither a strong two-bid nor a 2NT bid. Here the spade suit is too weak for 2♠. Open 1♠ and hope partner doesn't pass.
♠ A K Q 2 ♥ A K 6 4 ♦ 3 ♣ A 6 4 3	Here none of your suits has five cards. Open 1♣ and bid strongly next time.

9 pre-emptive bids

Suppose you are dealt a very strong hand. As you consider what bidding sequence will show your goodies to partner your tranquillity is rudely shattered when the opponent before you opens 3♠, taking away all your bidding space. Now you are going to have to guess what to do at a high level, and like any guess, you might get it wrong.

So what does a 3♠ opening bid mean? It is a nuisance bid!

You really can work it out

The idea is to deprive opponents who might hold strong hands of bidding space. Opening suit bids from 3♣ up to 5♦ are weak, called pre-emptive bids. They show:

- a long, strong suit, normally at least seven cards.

- few defensive tricks.

- no side 4-card major suit.

The idea of a pre-empt is to show a hand with considerable playing strength but with little value unless the suit is trumps. Because it takes up lots of space, opponents are left guessing. On the other hand, partner, who is the only player at the table to have an accurate picture of his side's total combined assets, is well placed to know what to do.

For safety, when you pre-empt you should expect to go down by no more than three tricks in your contract if you are not vulnerable, and by no more than two tricks if you are vulnerable, if partner produces a worthless dummy. This is known as the RULE OF 500, meaning that if you were doubled you would lose no more than 500 points.

♠ 4
♥ K Q J 8 5 4 3
♦ J 10 4
♣ 8 4

This hand is worth six tricks. Open 3♥ if not vulnerable, but pass if vulnerable.

♠ 4
♥ A Q 10 8 6 5 4
♦ Q 10 9 7
♣ 2

This hand is worth seven tricks (allowing one from diamonds). Open 4♥ not vulnerable or 3♥ if vulnerable. A four-level opening bid often has an 8-card suit, but a 7-card suit is sufficient if there is a source of tricks in a side suit.

♠ 4
♥ A K J 9 7 5 4 3
♦ J 10 9
♣ 8

This hand seems worth seven tricks, but eight are more likely. The ♥Q may drop and the diamonds may make two tricks opposite as little as ♦ K 3 2. Definitely a 4♥ opening. If your suit were a minor you would open 5♣ or 5♦.

♠ 8
♥ K Q J 10 8 4
♦ J 10 9 8 6
♣ 2

This hand has a side suit that might be worth tricks. Open 4♥ if not vulnerable or 3♥ if vulnerable.

♠ Q 10 9
♥ J 9 8 6 5 3 2
♦ A 7
♣ 8

This hand is not suitable for a pre-emptive opening bid. It has too weak a heart suit and too much defensive strength outside.

♠ Q 10 8 4
♥ A Q 10 8 7 6 5
♦ 2
♣ 6

With a 4-card spade suit, don't open 3♥. It would be foolish to go down in 3♥ with 4♠ a good contract. Once you have opened 3♥ partner will need a very good suit to investigate alternative trump suits.

If your partner opens with a pre-emptive bid, it is normal to play in his suit. Since his hand is weak, there will be few entries to the trick-taking potential of his suit unless that suit is trumps.

responding to a pre-empt

Suppose partner opens 3♠ with nobody vulnerable.

♠ 9 ♥ A K 7 3 ♦ A 9 3 2 ♣ A 7 4 2	Raise to 4♠. His six tricks plus your four make ten. It would be a serious error to try to play in no trumps because there would be few entries to partner's hand.
♠ A 10 7 2 ♥ 8 3 2 ♦ 9 3 ♣ K 9 4 2	Raise to 4♠. This time you don't expect to make it but you want to raise the stakes before your opponents discover they have an excellent fit in either or both the red suits.
♠ 9 ♥ K Q 3 2 ♦ K Q 3 2 ♣ K Q 3 2	Pass, despite your 15 points. Played in spades you expect to lose one trick in each suit. No trumps will fail because of lack of entries to cash spade winners. Aces and kings are useful, but not other honours.
♠ — ♥ K J 5 ♦ K Q 2 ♣ A K Q J 6 5 2	Bid 3NT. This time you don't need his spades. You hope to make seven clubs and the two red kings. He must not under any circumstances revert to 4♠.
♠ 3 2 ♥ — ♦ A K Q J 10 3 2 ♣ A Q 6 4	Bid 4♦. Any new suit below game is forcing and offers an alternative denomination to play.

Once a player has defined his hand with a pre-empt he NEVER bids again unless his partner invites him to do so. The partner of the pre-empter knows what is going on. He is in charge.

quiz on chapter 9

What do you open with these hands: (a) if you are not vulnerable, or (b) if you are vulnerable?

♠ K Q J 8 6 4 3 ♥ 9 7 ♦ J 7 2 ♣ 8	You have six tricks. Open 3♠ not vulnerable, pass if vulnerable.
♠ K Q 10 9 7 6 4 3 ♥ 7 ♦ Q 10 9 ♣ 2	Here you have about seven tricks. Open 4♠ if not vulnerable or 3♠ if vulnerable.
♠ K Q J 8 6 4 3 ♥ 9 7 ♦ A J 2 ♣ 8	This is too strong for a pre-empt. Open 1♠.
♠ K Q J 9 7 6 4 ♥ 9 7 ♦ Q J 10 8 ♣ −	You have about eight tricks. Open 4♠ at any vulnerability.
♠ A J 10 9 7 4 3 ♥ Q 10 9 6 ♦ 9 7 ♣ −	Not suitable for a pre-empt because it also contains a 4-card heart suit. Pass for now but come in strongly with spades later. Partner may work out why.
♠ K 8 7 6 4 3 2 ♥ A 3 2 ♦ J 8 ♣ 7	Pass. Not suitable for a pre-empt because the spades are weak and you have too much outside. In particular, this hand might play well in hearts if that is partner's suit.
♠ − ♥ 6 ♦ Q J 10 ♣ K Q J 10 9 7 6 4 3	Open 5♣ at any vulnerability. You don't get 9-card suits very often, but it is usually best to pre-empt.
♠ Q J 10 9 8 7 6 5 4 ♥ A K ♦ A K ♣ −	Open 5♠. This is not a pre-empt but asks partner to bid 6♠ with one of the ace or king or 7♠ with both of them.

With neither side vulnerable, your partner opens 3♥. What do you bid?

♠ A J 7 6 4 ♥ J ♦ A Q 4 2 ♣ A K 7	Raise to 4♥. 3NT would be a serious error because you are unlikely to have enough entries to partner's hand to use his heart suit.
♠ A Q 2 ♥ – ♦ A Q 2 ♣ K Q J 10 9 4 3	3NT. This time you expect to make 3NT without using his hearts. Partner *must* pass your 3NT. You are now in charge.
♠ 9 7 ♥ K 8 4 3 ♦ A Q 5 4 ♣ 6 4 2	4♥. It probably won't make, but put the pressure on your opponents before they bid and make 4♠.
♠ K Q 9 4 ♥ – ♦ J 7 5 4 ♣ A K Q J 10	Pass. Any attempt to improve things is likely to fail, leaving you too high and maybe doubled. In hearts, hope you can escape with the loss of a spade, two diamonds and a trump.
♠ A K 5 4 ♥ A 5 3 2 ♦ – ♣ K Q 5 3 2	6♥. Your wonderful shape, fit, and top cards make up for the lack of points. Surely the only trick you will lose is to the ♣A.
♠ A K J 10 4 3 ♥ – ♦ A K J 10 3 2 ♣ A	3♠. Natural and forcing. On the next round jump to 6♦, giving partner a choice between 6♦ and 6♠.

At love all, you open 3♥ and partner bids 3♠. What do you bid?

♠ 4 3 2 ♥ A J 10 9 8 3 2 ♦ 3 ♣ 3 2	4♠. This is an excellent hand in support of spades.
♠ 4 ♥ A J 10 9 8 3 2 ♦ 4 3 2 ♣ 3 2	4♥. With only one spade you must show you don't like spades by rebidding your suit.

10 bidding to slam

There is no greater pleasure for a bridge player than that which comes from bidding and making a slam. As a rough rule of thumb, you require 33 points for a small slam and 37 for a grand slam, although the hand seen in chapter 2 illustrates spectacularly that if you have a good fit and good shape you can often make a slam with far fewer points.

> The simplest way to bid a slam is to add your points to partner's known points total and if you reach the required number take the bull by the horns and bid it.

West	East	West	East
♠ A Q 7	♠ K 10 6	1NT	6NT
♥ K 8 3	♥ A 9 4		
♦ K 10 4	♦ A Q J 8		
♣ 10 8 4 3	♣ A Q J		

East has 21 points. Since West is known to have at least 12, a combined 33 points. East bids 6NT.

West	East	West	East
♠ A Q 7	♠ K 10 6	1NT	4NT
♥ K 8 3	♥ A 9 4	6NT	
♦ K Q 10	♦ A J 8 4		
♣ 10 8 4 3	♣ A Q J		

East has just 19 points. He invites 6NT by jumping to 4NT. With 14 points West is delighted to accept.

West	East	West	East
♠ A Q 8 7 5	♠ J	1♠	2♣
♥ K 7 3	♥ A Q J 10	2♠	6NT
♦ Q 5 3	♦ A J 10 9		
♣ J 8	♣ A K Q 6		

East starts with 2♣ to see if he can find a fit in clubs, diamonds or hearts but West disappoints him by rebidding 2♠. Knowing West is minimum, East gives up on a grand slam, but his 22 points should ensure 6NT.

the blackwood convention

If bidding and making a slam is the greatest pleasure in bridge, there can be few greater letdowns than bidding optimistically to a slam only to find that your opponents start by cashing two aces. If getting a minus score with good hands isn't hard enough to bear, their smug expressions are even worse.

To avoid such an indignity you can play the BLACKWOOD convention. It applies after you have agreed a trump suit. A bid of 4NT asks a question. 'How many aces do you have, partner?'

Over a 4NT bid asking how many aces you hold:

- 5♣ shows no ace or all four aces.

- 5♦ shows one ace.

- 5♥ shows two aces.

- 5♠ shows three aces.

Having heard your reply, partner can then either pick the final contract or continue with 5NT, which tells you all the aces are present and asks a further question. 'How many kings do you have, partner?'

Over a 5NT bid asking how many kings you hold:

- 6♣ shows no king or all four kings.

- 6♦ shows one king.

- 6♥ shows two kings.

- 6♠ shows three kings.

Bridge players love Blackwood, but it is often misused. Before using Blackwood check the following conditions apply.

- You know the final denomination.

- You are convinced that enough values for a slam are present. To fulfil a slam you need twelve tricks. Four aces stop the opponents taking the first two tricks, but that will be little comfort if you cannot make enough yourself.

- You can take the final decision as to the contract when you hear partner's answers. By using Blackwood you are taking control of the auction. Make sure you know what to do with the information.

Here are some hands where Blackwood is used correctly.

West	East	West	East
♠ A 7 4 3 2	♠ K Q J 6 5	1♠	4NT
♥ K 7 3	♥ 8	5♦	6♠
♦ 4 2	♦ A K Q J 10 9		
♣ K Q 4	♣ A		

East confidently jumps to 4NT. He knows spades will be trumps. If West shows one ace East will jump to 6♠, if West has two aces he can be certain of 7♠, or even 7NT.

You can bid a slam missing one ace. That might be the only trick you lose.

West	East	West	East
♠ K 10 9 6 5 4	♠ A 8 7 2	1♠	3♠
♥ A 6	♥ K 5 3	4NT	5♥
♦ A K Q 2	♦ 9 8	5NT	6♦
♣ 5	♣ A 6 3 2	7♠	

East's 5♥ shows two aces and the reply to 5NT shows a king. West can almost count thirteen tricks: six spades, the ♥A, ♣A, ♦ A K Q, the extra king and either a diamond ruff in dummy or a length trick in diamonds if East has four or more diamonds. The fact that East/West have just 27 points is irrelevant.

cue bidding

Sometimes you know you have sufficient values for a slam, but your worry is that the opponents will cash the first two tricks in a side suits. If you have agreed trumps and the bidding cannot stop below game, the bid of a new suit is called a CUE BID. The message is:

- I am interested in a slam, partner, but rather than take control of the auction with a Blackwood 4NT I want your co-operation.

- I have CONTROL of the suit I am bidding. If the suit is led, I can win the first trick, either with the ace or because I have a void and can trump.

- Please help me by showing which suit you similarly control. If you control two suits, start with the cheaper one.

West	East	West	East
♠ K 10 9 6 5 4	♠ A 8 7 3	1♠	3♠
♥ 9 3	♥ A 7 5 2	4♣	4♥
♦ A K Q 2	♦ 7 5	4NT	5♥
♣ A	♣ Q 10 5	5NT	6♣
		6♠	

West cue bids his first-round control in clubs. East co-operates by cue bidding the ♥A. Now West knows of the heart control he can use Blackwood. With all the aces present he bids 5NT. This is a try for a grand slam and it guarantees all the aces are present. Sadly, East doesn't have a king so West signs off in 6♠.

West	East	West	East
♠ K 10 9 6 5 4	♠ A Q 8 7	1♠	3♠
♥ 9 3	♥ Q J 7 4	4♣	4♠
♦ A K Q 2	♦ 7 5	5♦	5♠
♣ A	♣ Q 10 5		

Again West cue bids 4♣, but East denies a red ace by bidding 4♠. West continues with 5♦ to show control in diamonds. East realises West wants some control in hearts but he can't help.

quiz on chapter 10

Your partner opens 2NT. What do you bid with these hands?

♠ J 9 ♥ K 10 7 ♦ K 9 7 2 ♣ Q 8 3 2	3NT. Not strong enough for a slam try.
♠ J 8 ♥ A 10 8 ♦ K 9 7 2 ♣ A 10 6 5	4NT. 11-12 points, inviting 6NT.
♠ K 8 ♥ A 10 8 ♦ K 9 7 2 ♣ A 10 6 5	6NT. 13-16 points.
♠ A K ♥ A 10 8 ♦ K 9 7 2 ♣ A 10 6 5	7NT. 17 or more points.

Your partner opens 1♠ and rebids 2♠ over your 2♦ response. How do you continue with these hands?

♠ 7 4 ♥ A J 5 4 ♦ A Q 10 8 ♣ A J 8	3NT. Not strong enough for a slam try.
♠ J 7 ♥ A Q J 4 ♦ A K J 2 ♣ A J 8	6NT. No fit but plenty of points.

Over your 1♠ opening bid your partner jumps straight to 4NT. What do you bid with these hands: (a) now, and (b) if his next bid is 5NT?

♠ Q J 9 7 6 ♥ K 8 6 ♦ A 6 2 ♣ A 3	(a) 5♥. Two aces. (b) 6♦. One king.

♠ Q J 4 3 2 ♥ 7 ♦ K Q ♣ K Q 6 5 3	(a) 5♣. None or four aces. (b) 6♥. Two kings.
♠ A 8 4 3 2 ♥ A ♦ A 9 7 ♣ A 10 8 6	(a) 5♣. None or four aces. (b) 6♣. None or four kings.
♠ A 8 6 4 3 2 ♥ Q J 7 ♦ – ♣ K Q 4 3	(a) 5♦. One ace. You cannot show your void over Blackwood. (b) 6♦. One king.

What should you bid with these North hands after the auction:

South	North
1♥	1♠
3♠	?

♠ K Q 7 4 3 ♥ K 8 ♦ 7 ♣ A K Q 10 4	4NT, Blackwood. You are well equipped to take control. If no aces are missing, bid 7♠.
♠ K Q 7 4 3 ♥ A 8 ♦ 7 4 ♣ A K 10 4	4♣. A cue bid, hoping to hear 4♦. Don't Blackwood with two losing diamonds as you won't know what to do if one ace is missing.
♠ K 9 7 6 ♥ 8 ♦ K Q 10 6 ♣ Q J 4 2	4♠. A sign-off. Not enough for a slam.
♠ A J 8 6 5 ♥ A 8 ♦ 4 ♣ A Q 10 9 3	6♠. You have the values for this, and two aces cannot be missing.

What should you bid with these South hands after the auction:

South	North
1♥	1♠
3♠	4♣
?	

♠ Q J 7 3
♥ A K J 5 3
♦ 8 5
♣ K Q

4♥, showing first-round control in hearts and denying it in diamonds. Spades is the agreed trump suit.

♠ Q J 7 3
♥ K Q J 5 4
♦ 8 5
♣ A K

4♠. You have nothing to cue bid. Your ♣ A K may well be wasted because it sounds as if partner has a void in clubs.

♠ Q J 7 3
♥ A Q 5 4 3
♦ A Q 7
♣ 9

4♦. Cue bid your cheapest ace.

♠ Q J 7 3
♥ K Q 10 7 5 4
♦ —
♣ A Q 4

4♦. Cue bid your void.

Slam can be made on this pair of hands despite having just 23 points. How should it be bid?

♠ A K 10 9 6 5 3
♥ A
♦ K Q J 10 7
♣ —

```
  N
W   E
  S
```

♠ Q 8 7
♥ 10 9 4 2
♦ A 2
♣ 9 8 5 3

North	South
2♣	2♦
2♠	3♠
4♣	4♦
7♠	pass

North bids 4♣ to show club control. He is excited by South's 4♦, showing control in diamonds. If South's diamond control is the ace then North can count thirteen tricks. North correctly finishes the auction with 7♠. Note how vital the ♦A proves, while the ♣A would be useless. That is why using Blackwood would be an error.

11 overcalling their suit with your suit

Up to now you have been allowed to bid unhindered by opposition interference. Your decision on whether or not to open the bidding was based mainly on your point count. What if your opponents bid first? To see the difference, consider what action you might take with the following hands if your right-hand opponent opens 1♥.

♠ A 7 3
♥ A J 5 4
♦ A 9 2
♣ 8 4 3

Pass. You would have opened 1NT, but there is little point in bidding over an opposition 1♥. Opponents hold your best suit and your high cards are equally likely to take tricks whoever plays the hand.

♠ K Q J 10 9 8
♥ 8 2
♦ K 7 3
♣ 7 5

Bid 1♠. This hand is not an opening bid of 1♠ but you have strong reasons for wanting to make spades trumps. If spades are trumps your suit will be worth five tricks. If hearts are trumps your spades may not take a single trick, if one of your opponents has a singleton spade.

When opponents have opened the bidding first, your criteria for bidding change. You are less likely to have enough for game, and more likely to end up defending against their contract. You are thinking more along the following lines.

Don't pull faces because you're stuck for a bid

why overcall?

It is quite likely that each side can make its own contract.

This will usually be a part-score, but it is possible that each side can make game if it picks the trump suit. Sometimes opponents can make a high scoring contract, but if you outbid them you will escape relatively cheaply. Outbidding opponents to a contract that is likely to fail is called SACRIFICING. A hand like the one with ♠ K Q J 10 9 8 which is worth far more if you choose the trump suit, must compete aggressively.

You can push the opponents too high.

If you lose a part-score auction, you should aim to push your opponents to a slightly higher level than they would choose. They may have no problems in making 2♥, but if you can push them to 3♥ you give yourself the chance of a plus score.

Take up the bidding space and opponents may get to the wrong contract.

If you can cramp their bidding space the opponents may bid to the wrong contract. If they open 1♦ and you overcall 1♠ you have removed their 1♥ response and they might find it hard to find a 4-4 heart fit.

Help partner find the right lead.

If you lose the auction and partner has to make the lead you would like to give him some help. Suppose partner is on lead against no trumps and you hold that good spade suit. If you have bid spades along the way he will lead a spade. Otherwise, he will lead his own best suit.

While you want to overcall aggressively, you must exercise some caution, particularly if vulnerable, in case opponents double your overcall and you suffer an unpleasant penalty.

overcalling a suit

A suit overcall at the one level usually shows 8-16 points with a good suit of at least five cards. There is a way of judging the acceptability of a suit called the SUIT QUALITY TEST.

Count the number of cards in the suit. Add the number of honours, but only count the ten or the jack if there is a higher honour in the suit. The total is the SUIT QUALITY.

A Q J 7 4   has suit quality 8: 5 cards plus 3 honours.

A J 8 5 4 3   has suit quality 8: 6 cards plus 2 honours.

J 8 6 5 4 3   has suit quality 6: 6 cards but the jack doesn't count because there is no higher honour.

If you are considering a one-level overcall with minimum values (8, 9 or 10 points) your suit quality should be at least 7.

♠ A K J 10 9
♥ 8 5 2
♦ 9
♣ 10 9 7 5

Your right-hand opponent opens 1♦ at love all. Overcall 1♠. This is a minimum overcall, but your spades are excellent with suit quality 9. You badly want partner to lead a spade if he has to make the opening lead.

♠ Q 7 5 4 2
♥ A Q 3
♦ Q 5 4
♣ 7 2

Pass. This is two points stronger than the last hand, but your suit is poor with suit quality only 6. You don't particularly want to suggest a spade lead to partner. With borderline overcalls be influenced by the quality of your suit.

♠ Q 7 5 4 2
♥ A Q 3
♦ 6 5 4
♣ A K

Overcall 1♠. This time you have more points to make up for a poor suit.

♠ A K J 5 4　　Overcall 1♠. This is a maximum 1♠ overcall,
♥ 8 5 2　　　a full two aces stronger than it might be.
♦ A
♣ A 8 6 4

A suit overcall at the two level without a jump shows 10-18 points.
If you are considering such an overcall with 10 or 11 points your
suit quality should be at least 8.

♠ 6 3　　　　Suppose your right-hand opponent opens 1♥
♥ 7 4　　　　at love all. Over 1♥ this is a minimum 2♣
♦ K Q 2　　　overcall. You have 10 points, a 6-card suit and
♣ A J 8 7 4 3　suit quality 8.

♠ 9 3　　　　You have 11 points, a good 5-card suit and
♥ 8 4 3　　　suit quality 8. You want partner to lead a club.
♦ A 5 2　　　There is some risk of suffering a penalty, but,
♣ A Q J 9 8　not vulnerable, the gain outweighs the
　　　　　　　potential loss.

A suit overcall with a single jump shows 12-16 points and a good
6-card suit.

♠ A Q J 6 4 3　Your right-hand opponent opens 1♦ at love
♥ A 6　　　　all. This is normal for a 2♠ jump overcall. It
♦ 8 6　　　　has about six playing tricks. In an uncontested
♣ K 10 2　　auction you would open 1♠ and rebid spades
　　　　　　　with a jump.

♠ A 9　　　　Make a jump overcall to 3♣ over the opening
♥ K J 8　　　1♦. A jump overcall to the three level will tend
♦ 10 2　　　to be slightly stronger than to the two level.
♣ A K 10 9 4 3

A suit overcall with a double jump or higher shows a pre-emptive
hand. These bids are similar to 3♠ and 4♠ opening bids.

♠ A Q J 7 4 3 2   Not vulnerable,   ♠ A Q J 8 5 4 3 2
♥ 4 3   overcall a 1♦ opening   ♥ 4
♦ 9   bid with 3♠ with your   ♦ 9
♣ J 10 6   good 7-card suit or 4♠   ♣ J 10 6
                         with an eighth spade.

So what do you do if you have a hand suitable for an overcall but
stronger than any of these? You will find the answer in chapter 13.

responding to a one-level overcall

West	North	East	South
1♣	1♥	pass	?

What can South do after this start to the auction?

The responses by overcaller's partner tend to be simpler than
responding to an opening bid. Because both sides are active in
the auction, you may have less time to describe your assets, so
you should aim to get across a sharp and clear message.

Because North has at least five hearts for his overcall, 3-card
support is ample.

The point counts for heart raises are similar to raising an opening
1♥ bid.

♠ A 7 4 2   Partner overcalls the opening bid of 1♣ with
♥ K 7 3   1♥. Raise 1♥ to 2♥ showing about 6-9.
♦ 9 7 4 3
♣ J 10

♠ A K 4 2   Partner overcalls the opening bid of 1♣ with
♥ K 7 3   1♥. Raise 1♥ to 3♥ showing about 10-12.
♦ 9 7 4 3
♣ J 10

Be positive and aggressive with a fit but cautious with a misfit.

♠ A K 4 2	Partner overcalls the opening bid of 1♣ with
♥ K 7 3	1♥. Raise 1♥ to 4♥ showing at least 13
♦ 9 7 4 3	points or a very good distributional fit.
♣ A 10	

♠ 2	This hand is also worth a jump raise to 4♥ but
♥ K 7 5 4 2	for a different reason. Your shape and fit are
♦ 9 7 4 3	excellent and you may or may not make 4♥,
♣ A 7 3	but if you fail it is highly likely that your
	opponents could make 4♠. Pre-empt quickly
	before they find their spade fit!

Unless you have a fit with partner's overcall, don't respond with minimum values.

- Partner should have at least a good 5-card suit so you need not worry about passing with only one or two small cards in his suit.

- Since partner normally has at most 16 points you don't need to worry about missing game if you have 8 or fewer points.

- Try to find a bid with 9 points. Opposite the overcaller's maximum of 16 you are in the game zone.

- No trump responses to overcalls are considerably stronger.

♠ A 8 3 2	Partner overcalls the opening bid of 1♣ with
♥ 3	1♥. Respond 1NT showing 9-12 points
♦ J 9 8 5	
♣ A Q 9 4	

♠ A K 8	Respond 2NT showing 13-14 points. Because
♥ 3 2	the overcall can show as few as 8 points, you
♦ J 9 8 5	need at least 15 points to jump to 3NT. Of
♣ A Q 9 4	course, you need at least one stopper in their
	suit and preferably two. They have told you
	what they intend to lead, so be prepared for it.

After an overcall you should only change suit if you have reason to believe that your suit will play better than partner's, particularly if it involves raising the level of the contract.

West	North	East	South
1♣	1♥	pass	?

♠ K 8 6 4 3
♥ 8
♦ A 8 7
♣ 9 7 4 3

Pass. It is pointless fighting partner with hands like this.

Bridge is fun – make sure everybody enjoys it

♠ A Q J 7 5
♥ 8
♦ A 8 7
♣ 9 7 4 3

Respond 1♠.

♠ A 8 3
♥ 2
♦ K Q J 9 4 2
♣ 7 4 3

Respond 2♦. A simple change of suit is constructive but not forcing.

♠ A K 6
♥ 8
♦ K Q J 9 4 2
♣ K 6 2

Jump to 3♦. A change of suit with a jump is forcing.

responding to a two-level overcall

Use your common sense and judgement. Consider your bid after partner overcalls the opening 1♠ with 2♣.

♠ A 8 7 2
♥ 7 3
♦ A 6 3 2
♣ Q 10 3

Jump to 3NT. Your club fit means the club suit is likely to play for five or six tricks. You have a spade stopper and your ♦A will take a trick quickly. If a vital card like the ♣K is missing the bidding suggests the finesse will work. 3NT should succeed with a good long suit and top cards outside.

quiz on chapter 11

You are not vulnerable and your right-hand opponent opens 1♦. What should you bid with these hands? Work out the suit quality of your longest suit.

♠ 8 4 ♥ A 8 6 5 4 ♦ 10 3 2 ♣ K Q 2	Pass. Only 9 points and suit quality just 6.
♠ 8 4 ♥ A Q 6 5 4 ♦ 10 3 2 ♣ K 8 2	1♥. Still 9 points but suit quality 7.
♠ 8 3 ♥ K 6 3 ♦ 9 3 2 ♣ A K Q 7 2	2♣, showing 10-18 points. Suit quality is 8.
♠ J 8 ♥ A J 7 ♦ 9 3 ♣ A K Q J 6 3	3♣, showing 12-16 points and a good 6-card suit. Suit quality is 10.
♠ 3 ♥ K Q J 8 6 4 3 2 ♦ – ♣ J 10 9 6	4♥. A pre-emptive bid rather like a 4♥ opening bid. Suit quality is 11.
♠ A 2 ♥ K 8 6 5 4 3 2 ♦ 9 ♣ J 10 8	1♥. The suit is too weak for 3♥. Suit quality is 8.

What should South bid after the following start to the auction?

West	North	East	South
1♦	2♠	pass	?

♠ J 2 ♥ A J 7 3 ♦ A 6 4 ♣ J 9 4 2	4♠. North has a good 6-card suit. Play in the 6-2 major suit fit.

♠ — ♥ 10 4 3 2 ♦ K 7 ♣ A K Q J 7 5 2	3NT. You expect to make this with your solid clubs and diamond stopper. North must not bid 4♠.
♠ — ♥ K 8 7 5 4 ♦ 9 6 5 4 ♣ K 5 4 2	Pass. Don't fight partner with a weak misfit.
♠ 2 ♥ K Q J 10 8 6 5 4 ♦ 7 3 ♣ 6 2	4♥. The obvious contract.

What should South bid after the following start to the auction?

West	North	East	South
1♣	1♠	pass	?

♠ Q 6 3 ♥ A Q 3 2 ♦ A K 7 3 ♣ 7 3	4♠. 3-card support is quite sufficient.
♠ 2 ♥ K 7 3 ♦ A K Q 4 ♣ Q 10 9 7 4	2NT, showing a misfitting 13-14 points.
♠ 6 4 3 ♥ A 7 ♦ J 8 4 3 ♣ K 8 5 4	2♠, promising 6-9 points and at least 3-card support.
♠ 8 6 ♥ A Q 2 ♦ A J 10 9 8 5 ♣ 7 3	2♦. Constructive but not forcing.
♠ K 9 7 ♥ K 4 2 ♦ A K 7 5 4 3 ♣ 2	4♠. Don't bother to show your diamonds when you have good 3-card spade support.

♠ 8
♥ A J 2
♦ A K Q J 6 4
♣ 9 4 3

3♦. Forcing. If partner has a club stopper 3NT will probably be the best contract.

What should North rebid after the following start to the auction?

West	North	East	South
1♣	1♥	pass	2♦
pass	?		

♠ 8 5 3
♥ K Q J 10 4 3
♦ 8
♣ K 5 3

2♥. North has good hearts and doesn't like diamonds. This simple rebid suggests a minimum 1♥ overcall.

♠ A J 3
♥ K Q J 10 4 3
♦ K 2
♣ 7 4

3♥. A good overcall with a strong heart suit. 3♦ wouldn't be stupid as the diamond support is adequate, but it is more constructive to stress the self-supporting major suit.

♠ A K 3
♥ Q J 10 7 3
♦ 2
♣ 8 6 3 2

Pass. Don't fight partner.

♠ A 5 2
♥ A Q 6 4 3
♦ Q J 6 3
♣ 2

5♦. This is a wonderful hand if partner has strong diamonds.

Partner overcalls 1♠ with 2♣. What do you bid?

♠ A 4 3 2
♥ K Q 3 2
♦ K J 4 3
♣ 2

2NT (or pass). This is a misfit and partner will need a good overcall for game to make.

♠ A 4 3 2
♥ A 3
♦ J 10 4 3
♣ Q 10 2

3NT. Fewer points but it is easy to see that nine tricks are possible with the good club fit and aces as quick tricks.

12 no trump overcalls

♠ A 7 3	In chapter 11 you met this hand. It is an
♥ A J 5 4	obvious 1NT opening bid, but if your
♦ A 9 2	opponents start with 1♥ it really isn't worth
♣ 8 4 3	overcalling 1NT. Why?

■ There is no particular reason for you to want to play the hand because your high cards will take tricks equally as declarer or in defence.

■ Opponents find it much easier to double a 1NT overcall than a 1NT opening bid. Third hand knows partner has an opening bid, so he can easily tell when you have made a mistake. When 1NT is doubled and you find a worthless dummy, a large penalty can result. Not only are you outgunned in strength, but also you have no entries to dummy to take vital finesses.

Of course, as your balanced hand increases in strength there comes a point at which you cannot afford to pass because there is too great a possibility of missing game.

♠ A 7 3	Overcall 1♥ with 1NT, showing 16-18 points.
♥ A J 5 4	It is crucial that you hold at least one heart
♦ A 10 2	stopper, preferably two. A weak suit shouldn't
♣ K J 4	bother you, if there has been little bidding. However, if they have bid they have practically announced the intended lead.

♠ A 7 3	Overcall 1♥ with 2NT, showing 20-22 points,
♥ A J 5 4	including at least one stopper in the enemy
♦ A K J	suit. This is the same as a 2NT opening bid,
♣ K Q 4	and responses are the same. What do you do with 19 points? Wait for chapter 13.

♠ A K 3   Overcall 1♥ with 3NT. Despite your 26 points
♥ A J 5 4   you may fail if dummy has nothing, but all you
♦ A K Q   need is one card, maybe the ♠Q. You can't
♣ A J 10   expect a raise from 2NT to 3NT with just a
                 queen, so you must bid game yourself.

♠ 9 2   With this hand, a 3NT overcall is practical
♥ K 7   bridge. Of course, a spade lead could spell
♦ A 4   trouble, but you need to think positively in
♣ A K Q J 6 4 3 bridge. It's a pressure game. Give your
                 opponents difficult decisions and they will get
                 many of them wrong.

♠ K 7   Of course there are still hands that become
♥ J 6 3   very difficult to bid if opponents open. Over
♦ A Q 4 2   1♥, you can only pass. 1NT is out of the
♣ A Q 5 3   question without a heart stopper.

♠ A 8   When you have great strength in the opener's
♥ A Q J 9 8 4   suit as well as a very strong hand all you can
♦ 2   do is pass. What a pity it wasn't partner who
♣ K Q 6 5   opened 1♥! As it is, you should pass and
                 await developments. Why can't you double?
                 See chapter 13.

1NT overcall shows a balanced 16-18 points with a stop in the
suit opened.

2NT overcall shows a balanced 20-22 points with a stop in the
suit opened.

3NT overcall shows lots of points or a long running suit, with a
stop in the suit opened.

responding to 1NT overcall

This is exactly the same as responding to a 1NT opening bid, except that you need 4 points fewer for any constructive bid. Because the overcaller may be slightly less balanced than he would be for a 1NT opening bid, you should be cautious about insisting on a suit contract.

♠ K J 6 4 2
♥ 7 5
♦ A 7 3
♣ 10 5 2

If your partner overcalls a 1♥ opening bid with 1NT, jump to 3♠, looking for the 5-3 fit.

♠ 7 5 4 3 2
♥ J 6 2
♦ K 7 4
♣ 8 5

Pass partner's 1NT overcall. 2♠ wouldn't be wrong, but if partner has good clubs and a diamond guard you will regret not passing.

♠ 9 8
♥ 7 4 3
♦ J 7 3 2
♣ A K 5 2

Raise partner's 1NT to 2NT. This asks partner to bid on with a maximum.

♠ 5 4 2
♥ 7 3 2
♦ 6 3
♣ A K Q 4 2

Raise straight to 3NT and hope the clubs run for five tricks. Forget the idea of playing in the minor suit.

Say, 'Well done,' when your partner makes a contract.

quiz on chapter 12

Your right-hand opponent opens 1♠. What should you bid with these hands?

♠ A Q 2 ♥ A J 7 ♦ A J 10 7 6 ♣ A 4	2NT, showing 20-22 points. With two spade stoppers this describes your hand well.
♠ K Q 8 ♥ Q 9 7 5 4 ♦ A K 7 ♣ K 2	1NT, showing 16-18 points. The suit quality of your hearts is so poor that 1NT should be preferred to 2♥.
♠ 7 4 3 ♥ Q 9 7 5 4 ♦ A K Q ♣ A K	2♥. 1NT is unacceptable without a spade stopper, so despite the poor suit quality 2♥ is best.
♠ Q J 5 ♥ Q 2 ♦ A K Q J 6 3 ♣ J 4	1NT. Nobody could seriously criticise 2♦, but with a spade stopper and solid diamonds this is most likely to take you to a successful 3NT without the normal requirement of points.
♠ 7 4 3 2 ♥ A Q J ♦ A K Q ♣ J 4 3	Pass. What else?
♠ A 3 ♥ 9 ♦ A K Q J 10 6 4 ♣ J 8 3	3NT. A practical bid which will make far more often than not. Partner must realise you might have a spade stopper and a long solid minor and resist the temptation to bid 4♥.

You right-hand opponent opens 3♠. What do you bid?

♠ A Q 2 ♥ A J 7 ♦ A J 10 7 6 ♣ A 4	3NT. You bid only 2NT over 1♠ in the example above but over 3♠ you have to bid 3NT.
♠ Q J 5 ♥ Q 2 ♦ A K Q J 6 3 ♣ Q 4	3NT. Just hope partner has some useful cards. 3NT is much more likely to make than 4♦ or 5♦.

13 takeout doubles

♠ A 8
♥ A Q J 9 8 4
♦ 2
♣ K Q 6 5

You've seen this hand before. You were asked what action you should take if your right-hand opponent opens 1♥. Pass was suggested. So why can't you make a penalty double?

Ask yourself how often you will pick up a hand like this and hear an opponent open 1♥. Even if it does occur and you double for penalties, what will happen then? Much of the time they will escape into spades or diamonds. A penalty double of a suit opening bid is not a very useful weapon, and inevitably when this is the case expert players look for a more profitable use of the call.

♠ A Q 6 3
♥ 5
♦ Q 10 5 4
♣ A 9 8 7

Look at this hand. If an opponent starts with 1♥ you would like to pass the message to partner: 'We ought to be competing with this hand but I don't know which suit to pick. I would be happy with any of the other suits but I want you to choose.'

This sort of dilemma occurs far more frequently than a desire to double 1♥ for penalties, so bridge players give the double of a one-level suit opening bid a conventional use. It is called a TAKEOUT DOUBLE, requiring partner to 'take it out' by choosing one of the unbid suits.

The perfect shape for a takeout double is 4-4-4-1 or 5-4-4-0, having 4-card or better support for all the unbid suits. With this shape you can make a takeout double on 12 or more points.

Less ideal but more common shape is 4-4-3-2. Double with 13 or more points if your doubleton is in the opponent's suit.

Consider the hands below if opponents open 1♥.

♠ A Q 6 3 ♥ 5 2 ♦ A 10 5 4 ♣ K J 7	Double. You would prefer to hear spades or diamonds, but if partner chooses clubs it won't be a disaster.
♠ A Q 6 ♥ 2 ♦ A J 6 4 ♣ K 10 4 3 2	Double rather than bid 2♣. Admittedly partner, who will bid the unbid major suit if possible, will choose spades with four cards in each black suit, but double is more flexible than 2♣. You would hate to play in a 5-1 club fit with a 5-3 spade fit or 4-4 diamond fit available.
♠ K 10 4 3 2 ♥ 2 ♦ A J 6 4 ♣ A Q 6	The same hand with the black suits reversed. Now, with the high priority of finding the major fit, a 1♠ overcall is preferable to double. If you double you are unlikely to find a 5-3 spade fit.
♠ K 10 4 3 2 ♥ 2 ♦ A Q J 6 5 ♣ A 7	Can you double and, if partner bids clubs, continue with 2♦ to show the other two suits? No! Double followed by a change of suit shows a very strong hand. Here you overcall with 1♠ and hope to show diamonds later.
♠ A K J 6 4 ♥ 6 2 ♦ A K 7 ♣ A 5 2	If your right-hand opponent starts with 1♥ you are too strong for a spade overcall. The solution is to start with a takeout double. Let partner bid a suit and then you bid spades. This shows a strong hand.
♠ A Q 4 ♥ K J 2 ♦ A 9 8 ♣ K Q 5 2	Over 1♥, you are too strong for 1NT. Double and bid no trumps at your next turn. This shows the 19 point no trump overcall that you couldn't deal with earlier.

If you ask partner to choose and then overrule him, you are showing a very strong hand. In practice you start by doubling on most hands with 17 or more points.

bidding opposite partner's takeout double

If partner makes a takeout double he expects you to take it out!!! It is a grave lack of partnership discipline to pass just because you do not like your hand or because you have a headache.

How should South bid the hands below after

West	North	East	South
1♥	dbl	pass	?

♠ 8 5 3 2
♥ 6 4 3
♦ 7 4 2
♣ 9 8 2

Bid 1♠. It may not make – but you can't pass because you have a bad hand! 1♥ doubled will make with lots of overtricks, which will be far more expensive.

♠ K 7 3 2
♥ 9 4 2
♦ A J 6
♣ 10 5 3

Still bid 1♠. Bidding a suit at the cheapest level shows 0-8 points.

♠ K Q 3 2
♥ 9 4 2
♦ A J 6
♣ 10 5 3

Jump to 2♠. This shows 9-12 points but it is not forcing.

♠ K Q 3 2
♥ 9 4 2
♦ A J 6
♣ A 5 3

Game should be attempted and 4♠ is a sensible bid.

♠ 5 3
♥ K 10 9 3
♦ J 7 4 3
♣ K 8 2

Bid 1NT. South has been asked to choose a suit, but has a good enough holding in opener's suit to feel no trumps is best, even though the most likely holding for partner is a singleton. Bidding 1NT opposite a takeout double shows 6-9 points, like it does opposite an opening bid.

♠ A 5
♥ 10 8 3
♦ K J 7 4 3
♣ K 8 2

Jump to 3♦, showing 9-12 points. This is not a forcing bid. A jump to the three level in a minor suit suggests a 5-card suit because partner may only have three.

♠ A 5
♥ K 10 9 3
♦ J 7 4 3
♣ K 8 2

Bid 2NT, showing 10-12 points and a good stopper or two in hearts.

♠ A 5
♥ K J 10 9
♦ K 7 4 3
♣ K 8 2

Bid 3NT with better points and two definite heart stops.

Finally, a couple of hands that seem to break the rules.

♠ 7 4 3
♥ 8 6 5 4 2
♦ 6 4 3
♣ 10 5

East has been asked to pick a suit (apart from hearts) but he doesn't have one. He must improvise with 1♠.

♠ 9 6
♥ K Q J 9 8 7
♦ 8 5
♣ Q 3 2

This is the hand where East can justify passing 1♥ doubled. This is a positive choice to play in hearts, not because he doesn't fancy bidding. His hearts must be very strong! West is instructed to lead a heart (provided he has one).

Takeout doubles are to be taken out

which doubles are for takeout?

Having met the idea of a takeout double, you need to know when a double is for penalty and when for takeout.

West	North	East	South
1NT	dbl		

A double of no trumps is usually for penalty. This is dealt with in more detail in chapter 14.

West	North	East	South
1♠	pass	pass	dbl

Remember a double of an opening suit bid up to 3♠ is for takeout. The fact that it is in fourth position doesn't alter that principle.

West	North	East	South
1♥	pass	3♥	dbl

South doubles for takeout. He will have good shape and values to enter the auction at this level.

West	North	East	South
1♥	pass	2♣	dbl

South doubles for takeout, asking North to choose between the other two suits, spades and diamonds.

West	North	East	South
3♥	dbl		

North's double is for takeout, showing about a king more than a double of a one-level opening bid.

West	North	East	South
4♥	dbl		

After a four-level opening you may have to double on different hand types, from 16 points and short hearts to a 4-3-3-3 24 points. Partner often passes but will bid a good suit if he has one.

quiz on chapter 13

At game all, what do you bid with these hands if your right-hand opponent starts with 1♣?

♠ Q J 4 ♥ K 8 3 2 ♦ K Q 4 3 ♣ 7 4	Pass. Only 11 points and just three spades.
♠ A Q 4 ♥ K 8 3 2 ♦ K Q 4 2 ♣ 7 4	Double. Still only three spades but 14 points to compensate.
♠ A K 7 3 2 ♥ 9 4 3 2 ♦ A Q 9 ♣ 3	1♠. Your spades are so good that an overcall is better than a takeout double.
♠ A K 3 2 ♥ 8 5 4 3 2 ♦ A Q 9 ♣ 3	Double. With five very poor hearts and four good spades, allow partner to decide.
♠ A K 7 3 2 ♥ J 7 ♦ A K 2 ♣ A 8 4	Double. Too strong for 1♠. Bid spades next time.
♠ Q 2 ♥ 7 3 2 ♦ 8 3 ♣ A K Q J 9 5	Pass. You cannot make a penalty double.
♠ 7 4 3 2 ♥ A 8 3 2 ♦ A Q J 6 2 ♣ −	Double. Look for the major suit fit.
♠ A K Q 3 ♥ A K J 2 ♦ A Q J 8 ♣ 2	Double. There is no upper limit to a takeout double.

What should you bid with these hands after the following start to the auction?

West	North	East	South
1♣	dbl	pass	?

♠ Q J 7 3 2 ♥ A 4 ♦ Q 5 3 ♣ 8 4 2	2♠, showing 9-12 points.
♠ 6 4 2 ♥ A 8 7 ♦ Q 7 3 ♣ A J 10 9	2NT, showing 10-12 points and good club stoppers.
♠ K 10 3 2 ♥ 8 3 ♦ K 10 3 2 ♣ 10 4 3	1♠. When in doubt prefer the major suit.
♠ J 7 3 ♥ 8 3 2 ♦ 8 ♣ A K Q 9 8 7	Pass. This is a positive decision to choose clubs as trumps. Partner will lead a trump if he has one and you hope for blood.

What should you bid with these hands after the following start to the auction?

West	North	East	South
3♦	dbl	pass	?

♠ K J 4 3 2 ♥ A 7 3 ♦ 7 5 3 2 ♣ 3	4♠. More points and better shape than partner might expect.
♠ 8 4 3 ♥ K J 2 ♦ A 7 3 ♣ Q 4 3 2	3NT. Your diamond stopper should be sufficient if you hold up your ♦ A for the first two tricks. Pre-emptive hands rarely have outside entries.
♠ 6 3 ♥ A 5 3 ♦ Q J 10 9 ♣ 8 4 3 2	Pass, converting partner's takeout double to penalties. You have three defensive tricks.

14 competing over their 1NT

Doubles of no trump bids are usually for penalty rather than take-out. This makes sense, after all you can double a suit bid to show length in the other three suits but you can't have length in four suits!

To make a double of a 1NT opening bid you require about two more points than the maximum the 1NT bidder can have, namely 16.

Even then it is a risk. If opener's partner has most of the remaining strength and can redouble, you might be faced with the unpleasant choice of watching 1NT redoubled make with overtricks, or bidding a suit and being doubled for a substantial penalty. However, this is more than balanced by those delicious times when opener's partner has very little and you pick up a large penalty.

♠ K J 6 3
♥ A 2
♦ A K 7 4
♣ J 10 7

This is a typical minimum for doubling a weak 1NT opening. With a balanced hand you need at least 16 points to double.

♠ A
♥ 10 5 4 2
♦ K Q J 10 6 4
♣ K 6

It is also sensible to double with a long good suit, provided you are on lead. Despite the fact that you have only 13 points, you can envisage a very productive defence if you lead the ♦K. Hands where you have a solid suit, or a nearly solid suit together with outside entries, can destroy a no trump contract.

West	North	East	South
1NT	dbl	pass	?

South will usually pass. If he bids it will normally be because he is weak and fears that 1NT doubled will make. He must be cautious. Taking out partner's double of 1NT is not like signing off opposite a 1NT opening bid, since partner's hand may not be balanced.

♠ 8 5 2
♥ 6 3 2
♦ 9 6
♣ J 8 7 4 3

Here it is reasonable to bid 2♣. If partner has a good suit he can bid it and you will pass.

♠ J 8 7 4 3
♥ 9 4 2
♦ 8 5 3
♣ 7 2

However, you should pass here because a 2♠ sign-off would push the bidding too high. Not only might you suffer a penalty from 2♠ doubled, but you might find that partner could have beaten 1NT doubled single-handed.

♠ K Q J 7 5 4 2
♥ 6 3
♦ 5 4 2
♣ 8

Bid 4♠. You have no reason to believe partner will have enough in spades to make any use of your hand, or that he will ever be persuaded to lead spades.

♠ K J 7
♥ K 6 2
♦ K 4 3
♣ 10 8 4 3

Of course, this is South's dream hand. He passes and awaits with pleasure declarer's horror when dummy appears with nothing!

West	North	East	South
1NT	dbl	2♠	?

If opener's partner bids over the double, a bid by South is constructive but not forcing, maybe with 5-7 points.

♠ 8
♥ K 7 3
♦ 6 5 2
♣ Q 10 8 6 5 4

After this start to the auction South bids 3♣, but if he is stronger he must either jump or perhaps bid the enemy suit, 3♠.

Bidding the enemy suit is rather like bidding the fourth suit in an uncontested auction, conventional, forcing and asking for partner's help.

♠ A Q 9 2	South hopes that East has jumped out of the
♥ Q 7 3	frying pan into the fire and doubles for
♦ 8 5	penalties. Once 1NT has been doubled a
♣ 7 4 3 2	simple rule is to play that all subsequent
	doubles are for penalties.

overcalling 1NT with a suit

An overcall of 1NT denies as many as 16 points, because with that strength you would have doubled. You must remember that your overcall is at the two level so the suit quality for a two-level overcall described in chapter 11 must apply. Indeed, if you do overstep the mark, opener's partner might be in an even better position to double for penalties because he knows opener is balanced.

♠ K 7	This is a sensible minimum for a 2♥ overcall,
♥ K J 10 5 4 3	both in terms of strength and suit quality.
♦ Q J 5	
♣ 7 4	

♠ A K	Whilst this is too strong for a 2♥ overcall, a
♥ K J 10 5 4 3	penalty double should, hopefully, be
♦ A Q 3	profitable. If partner or opponents bid, you can
♣ 7 2	bid your heart suit.

quiz on chapter 14

Your right-hand opponent opens 1NT, showing 12-14 points. What do you do with these hands?

♠ K J 4 3 ♥ A Q 2 ♦ K 6 4 ♣ Q 4 3	Pass. You have 15 points, one more than the maximum that the 1NT bidder can have, but it is not quite enough to double and there is no other bid that can even be considered.
♠ A 4 ♥ 7 4 ♦ 8 4 2 ♣ A K Q J 7 6	Double. Only 14 points but you should take the first seven tricks even if your partner has nothing.
♠ Q 7 4 3 2 ♥ A J ♦ K J 6 ♣ Q 10 2	Pass. You have an opening bid but the suit quality of your spades is not remotely good enough to overcall 2♠.
♠ K Q 10 9 4 3 ♥ K 5 3 ♦ A K ♣ Q 9	Double. This is too strong for 2♠. All hands with 16 or more points start with a penalty double.
♠ A Q 10 9 5 3 ♥ A 10 7 ♦ 8 7 6 ♣ 3	2♠. You have a good 6-card suit and are not strong enough to double.
♠ K J 8 3 ♥ A Q 3 ♦ A J 2 ♣ Q 4 2	Double. You don't have a particularly good opening lead but you are 3 points stronger than the opener's maximum for 1NT.

What should South bid after the bidding sequences shown?

West	North	East	South
1NT	dbl	pass	?

♠ 7 4 3 ♥ 8 2 ♦ J 10 9 4 3 2 ♣ 8 6	2♦. A very weak hand but a respectable suit.
♠ K 4 2 ♥ K Q 3 2 ♦ A 7 4 ♣ 10 9 6	Pass, with relish!
♠ K Q J 10 7 6 4 ♥ – ♦ J 4 3 2 ♣ 7 6	4♠. Partner won't lead spades against no trumps. Just bid your game.

Same hands, different sequence. What should South bid this time?

West	North	East	South
1NT	dbl	2♥	?

♠ 7 4 3 ♥ 8 2 ♦ J 10 9 4 3 2 ♣ 8 6	Pass. To bid 3♦ would be constructive, showing a better hand than this.
♠ K 4 2 ♥ K Q 3 2 ♦ A 7 4 ♣ 10 9 6	Double, for penalties.
♠ K Q J 10 7 6 4 ♥ – ♦ J 4 3 2 ♣ 7 6	4♠. It's even more obvious now to bid game and show your very good suit.

15 partner opens, opponents intervene

When opponents intervene after your partner's opening bid it would be foolish to pretend that you can carry on bidding regardless. Their intervention will have given you new problems and fresh opportunities and your bidding should be modified to take account of this.

partner's 1♥ is doubled

The takeout double has taken away none of your bidding space and has given you two extra options.

- you can redouble.

- you don't need to strain to bid on a poor 6 points. The double has given partner another chance to call.

Let's start by considering how we might use the redouble. An opponent has made a takeout double. There is risk in this. As with any intervention he will sometimes find his partner with a weak, misfitting hand and then they might suffer a nasty penalty. Responder should be on the lookout for opportunities to exploit this.

Redouble is a conventional bid to announce at least 10 points and the prospect of a penalty.

Redouble says your side has the balance of power, so either you should buy the contract yourself or double them.

♠ A J 10 2
♥ 7
♦ K J 10 4
♣ Q J 9 8

A perfect redouble if your partner's 1♥ is doubled. You don't like partner's hearts, which means that his heart tricks are likely to score in defence. You want to double whatever contract your opponents bid. Don't worry that 1♥ redoubled will be passed out. If it is, your partner would make it through brute strength!

♠ K J 10 2
♥ 8 3
♦ A Q 9 7
♣ 9 6 2

Of course such perfect hands for a redouble are few and far between. A more likely hand is this one, where you can double spades or diamonds and hope partner can double clubs.

Here are examples of how the bidding might develop

♠ 7 4 3
♥ A K Q 7 4
♦ 6
♣ A 10 4 3

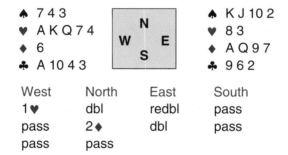

♠ K J 10 2
♥ 8 3
♦ A Q 9 7
♣ 9 6 2

West	North	East	South
1♥	dbl	redbl	pass
pass	2♦	dbl	pass
pass	pass		

West passes on the second round and North rescues to 2♦. East doubles for penalties. Note that if North had rescued to 2♣, East would have passed and West would have doubled.

♠ 7 4 3
♥ A K Q 7 4
♦ K 6 4 2
♣ 3

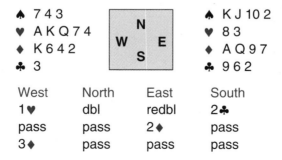

♠ K J 10 2
♥ 8 3
♦ A Q 9 7
♣ 9 6 2

West	North	East	South
1♥	dbl	redbl	2♣
pass	pass	2♦	pass
3♦	pass	pass	pass

West cannot double 2♣ so leaves it to East. East doesn't have the trumps to double 2♣ but must not pass because West may be quite strong. East bids 2♦, which is forcing. West's raise to 3♦ ends the bidding.

> Remember that to double a low-level enemy contract for penalties you need good trumps!

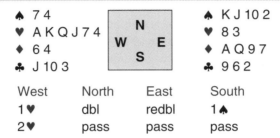

	♠ 7 4		♠ K J 10 2
	♥ A K Q J 7 4		♥ 8 3
	♦ 6 4		♦ A Q 9 7
	♣ J 10 3		♣ 9 6 2

West	North	East	South
1♥	dbl	redbl	1♠
2♥	pass	pass	pass

West doesn't give East the chance to double. West only opened because of his long, strong hearts. He has far less defensive strength than East will expect. Bidding 2♥ shows this.

bidding with a fit for partner

After an opponent's double, if you have a misfit with partner you look for opportunities to double opponents. Conversely, if you have a good fit you should be prepared to raise the level of bidding in order to make it hard for your opponents to find their fit. Remember, the better the fit you have, the better the fit they will have.

The auction starts as shown below.

West	North	East	South
1♥	dbl	?	

♠ 8 4   Raise to 2♥ because you would be happy to
♥ Q 7 4 2   buy the contract in 2♥.
♦ J 10 7 5
♣ 7 3 2

♠ 8 4
♥ Q 7 4 2
♦ A J 9 5
♣ 7 3 2

Jump raise to 3♥. Without the double you would only bid 2♥. You don't want opponents to get together, so bid as high as you dare immediately and hope they misguess.

♠ 7 4
♥ K 8 5 4 3 2
♦ Q J 10 5
♣ 3

With really long hearts and poor defence, jump to 4♥.

2♥, 3♥ and 4♥ are all pre-emptive raises, higher than you would have bid without the double.

♠ 8 4
♥ Q 7 4 2
♦ A K J 2
♣ 7 4 2

A genuine raise to 3♥ is shown by a 2NT bid. 2NT is not really necessary to show a balanced hand of 10-12 points because you redouble with that hand.

Finally, we look at some hands where you don't know of any great fit with partner, but you don't see much prospect of penalising opponents. Suppose partner opens 1♥ and the next hand doubles.

West	North	East	South
1♥	dbl	?	

♠ J 7 3 2
♥ 6 2
♦ Q 9 5 4
♣ K Q 6

Respond 1NT, which shows 7-9 points after the double. With fewer points you would pass.

♠ K Q 9 8 2
♥ 8 6 2
♦ K 6 2
♣ 8 4

Bid 1♠, natural and forcing and implying quite good spades.

♠ A K J 10 7 4
♥ A K 2
♦ 9
♣ 8 4 3

Jump to 2♠, a game-forcing jump shift.

opponents overcall
your partner's opening bid

West	North	East	South
1♣	1♠	?	

How have East's options been altered by North's 1♠ overcall in this auction?

■ he cannot respond 1♦, 1♥ or for that matter 1♠.

■ he has extra bids with double or even with a bid of their suit, 2♠ (a concept you will meet later).

■ he cannot respond in no trumps without a spade stopper.

■ he might want to penalise 1♠ with a penalty double, particularly if he has a misfit with his partner.

Often, East can just ignore the overcall.

♠ 9 4 2 ♥ 7 4 ♦ A J 7 3 ♣ Q 7 3 2	East raises to 2♣, as before. If the hearts were A 4 instead of 7 4, he would bid 3♣.
♠ 6 4 3 ♥ A Q J 7 3 ♦ 8 2 ♣ A 8 3	A new suit over the overcall is natural and forcing, so East can respond 2♥ with 9+ points and a 5-card or longer suit.
♠ 6 4 3 ♥ A 7 6 3 ♦ Q 7 5 2 ♣ K 4	This is a hand where you are really inconvenienced by the overcall. You would have responded to 1♣ with 1♦, but you really cannot stretch to a forcing 2♦ or 2♥. You might pass and wait for partner to bid, but all too frequently South will raise the stakes to 2♠ or 3♠ and you will have an even harder problem next time.

The solution is to play that double shows this sort of hand, where your bid has been stolen. It is for takeout (sometimes called a negative double). In particular, when there is just one unbid major suit double shows that major.

Takeout doubles of an opponent's overcall are a relatively new idea, but it is far more likely that you hold this sort of hand than a hand suitable for a penalty double. Moreover, if you do want to make a penalty double you will see below that you still have a way! Double is just like a 1♥ response, and opener rebids just as he would if the auction had started:

West	North	East	South
1♣	1♠	1♥	

Convenient, isn't it!

So what does East do if he would like to make a penalty double of 1♠? Look at this hand:

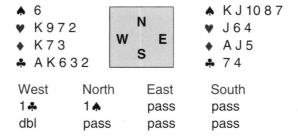

♠ 6		♠ K J 10 8 7
♥ K 9 7 2		♥ J 6 4
♦ K 7 3		♦ A J 5
♣ A K 6 3 2		♣ 7 4

West	North	East	South
1♣	1♠	pass	pass
dbl	pass	pass	pass

East passes the 1♠ overcall! His partner is almost certain to be short in spades and if this is the case West will re-open the bidding with a double. This double is for takeout (because East had not made a bid) but East is only too happy to leave it in.

If East was not happy to pass a re-opening double he could jump to 2NT straight away, showing 10-12 points and spade stops.

Finally, we don't want to burden you with lots of sequences to memorise, but it is worth while looking at some more takeout doubles. Try to work out by common sense what East has for these sequences:

West	North	East	South
1♣	1♥	dbl	

West	North	East	South
1♣	1♥	1♠	

With the double, East shows the unbid major. That means that a 1♠ bid shows five spades.

West	North	East	South
1♣	1♦	dbl	

West	North	East	South
1♦	2♣	dbl	

When there are two unbid majors, a double of 1♦ shows them. But if the bidding is higher the double is a general takeout bid.

West	North	East	South
1♥	1♠	dbl	

West	North	East	South
1♥	2♠	dbl	

Where there is no unbid major, East has both minors. East should have extra values for a takeout double at the two level.

Takeout doubles of overcalls are played up to a 2♠ overcall. The higher the overcall, the fewer options you have, so the greater the need for flexibility.

opponents overcall your partner's opening bid with 1NT

This is relatively easy. You need points to double no trumps. The 1NT overcall might show 16-18 points but if opener's partner is strong the overcaller might suffer a very nasty penalty, particularly if he cannot reach dummy to take vital finesses.

West	North	East	South
1♣	1NT	?	

♠ A J 7
♥ J 10 9 3
♦ K J 4 2
♣ 7 4

East doubles, as he would do with almost any hand with 10 or more points.

♠ 5 3
♥ K Q 10 9 3 2
♦ 8 3
♣ 9 3 2

East can bid 2♥. This shows a good suit but is not forcing. East's failure to double 1NT limits his strength to about 9 points.

Learn from the mistakes of others – you won't live long enough to make them all yourself

quiz on chapter 15

What should you bid with these hands after the following start to the auction?

West	North	East	South
1♥	dbl	?	

♠ J 8
♥ K 8 4 3
♦ 8 7 5 2
♣ 10 8 4

2♥. This shows 4-card heart support and values that would not have warranted a raise without the double.

♠ A 8
♥ K 8 4 3
♦ K 8 7 5
♣ 10 8 4

2NT. Conventional, showing a raise to 3♥.

♠ 7
♥ K 8 5 4 3
♦ K 10 9 7 3
♣ 7 4

4♥. Pre-empt before they bid and make 4♠.

♠ A Q 9 8
♥ Q 8 4 2
♦ 8 4
♣ 7 4 3

3♥. A good raise to 2♥ without the double.

♠ A Q J 9 8
♥ 8 4
♦ 10 7 4
♣ 8 7 3

1♠. It is likely that North has four spades for the double but East's suit is far too good to suppress.

♠ A Q 9 8
♥ 8 4
♦ K J 10 8
♣ 6 4 3

Redouble. East will double spades or diamonds and hopes West can double clubs.

♠ 7 4 2
♥ 8 6
♦ K 8 3 2
♣ Q J 7 5

Pass. East doesn't have to strain to bid on a misfitting 6 points because West gets another bid.

♠ Q 10 4
♥ 8 4
♦ K 8 4 3
♣ Q J 9 7

1NT, showing 7-9 points.

What should you rebid after this start to the auction?

West	North	East	South
1♥	dbl	2NT	pass
?			

♠ 6 4
♥ A Q 7 4 3
♦ K 7 2
♣ Q J 7

3♥. A minimum 1♥ opening bid.

♠ A 7
♥ A Q 7 4 3
♦ K 7 3
♣ Q J 7

4♥. Easily worth game opposite a good raise to 3♥.

How should you continue if the auction starts like this?

West	North	East	South
1♥	dbl	redbl	1♠
pass	pass	?	

♠ A Q J 7
♥ 7 5
♦ K J 10 9
♣ 9 4 2

Double, for penalties!

♠ 8 4 2
♥ 7 5
♦ K J 10 9
♣ A Q J 7

2♣. Partner cannot double spades, and you certainly can't. You must find another bid. 2♣ is forcing.

♠ 8 7 6 5
♥ A Q 2
♦ K J 10 3
♣ 4 3

2♥. Although you have four spades they are very weak. Better to show support for partner. You can't have four hearts or you would have raised the round before.

♠ 8 7 6
♥ A Q 2
♦ A Q J 2
♣ 4 3 2

3♥. As above, you will only have three hearts. Your 13 points make up for the trump length.

How should you respond with the hands below after this start to the auction?

West	North	East	South
1♦	1♠	?	

♠ 7 4 ♥ K J 7 3 ♦ K 10 4 2 ♣ 8 4 2	Double, showing four hearts. Best to show the major before supporting diamonds.
♠ 7 4 ♥ K J 7 3 ♦ K 10 4 2 ♣ A Q 3	Double. Stronger this time, but there is no upper limit to a takeout double. Show the extra strength next time.
♠ 7 4 ♥ A Q J 6 5 ♦ K 7 3 ♣ J 6 2	2♥. Forcing and guaranteeing five hearts.
♠ 7 4 ♥ Q J 9 6 5 ♦ K 7 3 ♣ 9 6 2	Double. This doesn't show the fifth heart but the hand is too weak for a forcing 2♥.
♠ A Q 2 ♥ 9 7 2 ♦ Q 7 3 ♣ K 8 4 3	2NT. This is natural, showing 10-12 points with at least one spade stopper. It doesn't promise a diamond fit.
♠ 9 2 ♥ A 9 7 ♦ Q 7 4 3 2 ♣ 7 5 3	2♦. Bid normally over the overcall. You would have raised 1♦ to 2♦ if North had passed.
♠ A Q 10 9 5 ♥ K 8 4 ♦ 6 4 ♣ 10 9 4	Pass. Hope that West, who surely has short spades, will re-open the bidding with a takeout double, which you will be delighted to pass.
♠ 8 5 4 3 ♥ A 7 2 ♦ Q 4 ♣ Q 9 4 3	Pass. You have nothing to say. If West is strong he will bid again.

16 protective bidding

Earlier you saw hands that were worth a bid but for which there was no sensible course of action if your opponents opened first, for example, a balanced 15 points. Clearly if both partners adopt this approach there is a danger that opponents will go several off at the one level, giving you inadequate compensation for a missed game. Playing duplicate pairs where every hand is of equal importance irrespective of whether it is in the slam score or a humble part-score, you cannot allow opponents to steal part-score contracts.

The solution is for the fourth hand, called the PROTECTIVE hand because he needs to protect his partner, to be more adventurous.

Consider South's actions after this start to the auction.

West	North	East	South
1♦	pass	pass	?

If South is weak he knows that North has some values, otherwise why would East and West be passing out 1♦? He can bid on comparatively sparse values without any real risk. Since it is quite likely that each side has half the points, South must try very hard to find a bid. As a rule of thumb, for most minimum bids he mentally adds 3 points to his assets and if the hand would then seem to be worth a bid he makes that bid. This is often called the 'borrowed king'.

♠ Q 7 5 3 2   South can bid 1♠. The hand is poor and the
♥ K 6 2   suit quality feeble, but North must have some
♦ 8 7   points, possibly as much as a balanced hand
♣ A 6 4   with 15 points.

♠ A Q 10 6 2
♥ 8 5
♦ 7 4
♣ J 10 9 4

This is also worth 1♠, the extreme weakness being balanced by the good suit and the desire to have a spade lead if you lose the auction.

♠ K 7 4 3
♥ A 7 3 2
♦ 7
♣ K 10 4 3

Make a takeout double with short diamonds on 10 points or more.

♠ Q J 6
♥ K 7 2
♦ A Q 7
♣ 10 9 4 2

1NT shows 12-14 points in the protective position, not the normal 16-18 needed for a 1NT overcall. You are bidding some of partner's values.

♠ A J 7
♥ K 3 2
♦ 10 4 2
♣ A 6 4 3

Rather surprisingly, this is also a 1NT bid. It may seem like heresy to suggest bidding no trumps without a diamond stopper. Often, North will have a diamond stopper, and if not, it isn't fatal to a contract of 1NT if you lose the first four or five diamond tricks.

♠ 7 2
♥ 10 6 3
♦ A Q J 7
♣ A 5 3 2

Pass with too many values in diamonds. Partner is probably short in diamonds so is unlikely to be very strong given his pass over 1♦. Your opponents are probably in a silly contract, don't give them a chance to escape.

If South is adding 3 points, North must subtract 3 points, otherwise the partnership will repeatedly get too high. North must be constantly aware that South is bidding his hand for him, so he should not punish South for being enterprising in the bidding.

Consider North's response to South's protective takeout double.

West	North	East	South
1♦	pass	pass	dbl
pass	?		

♠ A J 5 2   1♠ is quite enough. Subtracting 2 points
♥ 9 8 5   makes just 7 points, not enough for 2♠.
♦ Q 6 4
♣ Q 6 2

♠ 6 5 2   1NT is quite enough.
♥ Q 8 5
♦ A Q 4 3
♣ K 6 2

In the sequence below North has to decide whether to enter the auction.

West	North	East	South
1♦	pass	2♦	pass
pass	?		

Now North must commit himself at the two level if he wishes to compete, but it is even more essential to be aggressive. If East/West have found a fit but are still passing the hand out at a low level, not only is South known to have some points but it is certain that North/South also have a fit somewhere. It is very likely that they can make 2♦, while you can make at least eight tricks in the suit of your fit. At the very least you must try to push them one level higher where they might fail.

♠ J 10 5 2   Protect with a takeout double, despite only
♥ Q 8 5 2   having 9 points. You have borrowed a king
♦ 3   from partner.
♣ A Q 5 3

quiz on chapter 16

What should you bid after the following start to the auction?

West	North	East	South
1♥	pass	pass	?

♠ 5 3 ♥ A 4 2 ♦ K 7 3 2 ♣ K Q 10 7	1NT, showing 12-14 points in the protective position.
♠ Q 10 5 4 ♥ 7 4 ♦ K 7 6 ♣ A 6 3 2	Double, for take-out.
♠ A Q J 6 4 3 ♥ 3 ♦ A Q 10 ♣ 6 4 2	2♠. This still shows a good 6-card suit and 12-16 points because it is not a minimum bid.
♠ A 2 ♥ A 6 3 ♦ K 10 5 4 ♣ K Q 3 2	Double. This is too strong for 1NT which would show 12-14 points. Over the likely 1♠ response continue with 1NT.

How should you respond to partner's protective 1♠?

West	North	East	South
1♦	pass	pass	1♠
pass	?		

♠ Q J 4 ♥ A K ♦ K 8 7 ♣ J 8 5 4 3	3♠. Remember, South may be weak for his 1♠ protective overcall. Subtract 3 points and the hand isn't worth game if partner is minimum.
♠ 7 ♥ K 7 2 ♦ A J 7 2 ♣ 8 5 4 3 2	Pass. Subtract 3 points and you have just 5 points, which is not strong enough for 1NT opposite a 1♠ overcall.
♠ 6 ♥ A 9 7 ♦ A K 6 5 ♣ J 9 7 4 3	1NT. Subtract a king and you have 9 points, just right for a 1NT response to an overcall which shows 9-12 points.

17 using judgement

This final chapter shows you how your judgement will develop as you gain experience.

Many thousands of bridge players know the theory outlined in this book. So why are they not all equally good? What makes a world champion player?

One of the features that distinguishes the expert from the ordinary player is judgement. Bridge is not just a list of rules to be obeyed: it is far more exciting than that! There are many hands that don't fit any bid and you must try to choose the one which distorts least. For example, what do you open with

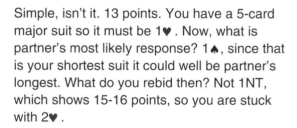

♠ A 4	Simple, isn't it. 13 points. You have a 5-card
♥ 7 5 4 3 2	major suit so it must be 1♥ . Now, what is
♦ A Q 4	partner's most likely response? 1♠, since that
♣ K 6 4	is your shortest suit it could well be partner's
	longest. What do you rebid then? Not 1NT,
	which shows 15-16 points, so you are stuck
	with 2♥ .

Not very attractive, is it. Maybe your choice of opening bid is not that simple after all! You won't be too surprised to learn that many experts will anticipate this turn of events and open 1NT, treating the hearts as a 4-card suit. Guidelines must first be mastered, but then they should be your servant not your master.

You have been told to raise partner's suit only with 4-card support or better, but sometimes it is right to raise with just three cards.

♠ 3
♥ A 3 2
♦ 9 5 4 3 2
♣ K 8 6 2

Partner opens 1♥. You don't want to pass with 7 points. You don't fancy 1NT with a spade singleton. Best is to raise to 2♥, hoping partner has five hearts. If partner only has four hearts he will usually have 15 or more points.

♠ 3
♥ A K Q
♦ 9 4 3 2
♣ K J 8 6 2

Similarly as opener you bid 1♣ and partner responds 1♥. The book rebid is 2♣ but a raise to 2♥ may well be more encouraging to partner. If partner looks upset when dummy goes down, put the ♦2 in with the hearts!

In the field of overcalling, rules are made to be broken. Suppose your right-hand opponent starts with 1♣ and you have this hand.

♠ 3
♥ A K Q J
♦ 9 4 3 2
♣ K 8 6 2

A 1♥ overcall is practical bridge. Admittedly you don't have a 5-card heart suit, but if your partner is on lead against an enemy contract you certainly want a heart lead and you won't come to much harm if partner raises your hearts with 3-card support.

Rules for pre-empting are there to help you, not put you in a strait-jacket. Suppose at love all you are third to speak, your partner and right-hand opponent having already passed.

♠ 7 3	With either, a 3♦ opening	♠ 8
♥ J 7 3 2	makes sense, despite your	♥ 3 2
♦ K Q J 10 5 4 3	4-card heart suit in one	♦ A Q J 10 5 4 3
♣ –	and your opening values in	♣ K Q 4
	the other.	

The idea is to make opponents' life difficult. Your left-hand opponent may well have the strongest hand at the table, so make life hard for him.

The higher the level of bidding, the more improvisation is necessary. What should you bid if your left-hand opponent opens with a pre-emptive 3♥ and it is passed round to you? The pre-empt was meant to make life hard for you and it has succeeded! In each case you could bid a virtuous 4♣, but that rules out any possibility of playing in 3NT. With solid clubs don't you feel that 3NT is likely to be the right contract?

♠ 7
♥ K 7 2
♦ A 3 2
♣ A K Q J 6 4

3NT is the practical bid! Of course spades may be a problem, but they won't necessarily lead spades.

♠ A 2
♥ K
♦ 8 4 3
♣ A K Q J 7 5 2

Again, bid 3NT. It is more than likely that the opening leader has the ♥A, but you don't think he is likely to lead it, do you? He is far more likely to underlead it in order to maintain communication with his partner's hand. That will allow you to take trick 1 with your singleton ♥K.

In both cases you are improvising. Improvisation can go wrong, and sometimes does so, even if you are a world champion. A good partner will be tolerant and understanding.

Judgement also involves upgrading points that seem to be useful and downgrading others. You have already seen that singleton kings are unlikely to be worth 3 points, but as the auction develops you might change your mind.

If you are dealt the singleton ♥K your first reaction is to be cautious. If partner opens 3♥ suddenly it becomes a vital card. Conversely, if your left-hand opponent opens 3♥ it is likely to be little more than waste paper. If your right-hand opponent opens 3♥ it might be a useful defensive card, taking a trick on a finesse, but it will probably be useless if you or your partner play the hand.

As the auction develops you should be ready to change your mind about your hand. How has your opinion of the hand held by West altered as a result of the bidding sequence shown?

West	North	East	South
1♠	pass	2♣	pass
?			

♠ A Q J 6 4 3
♥ A 10 2
♦ 8
♣ Q 5 4

If East has a poor club suit he might have chosen some other response, so suppose he has ♣ K J 7 4 2. Your club holding will be most welcome. Stretch to a 3♠ jump rebid.

♠ A Q J 6 4 3
♥ A 10 2
♦ Q 5 4
♣ 8

Now your singleton club will do nothing to enhance the trick-taking capacity of partner's suit. A rebid of 2♠ is sufficient.

The higher the level of bidding, the greater the need for judgement. What should West say next in the auction below? Both sides are vulnerable.

West	North	East	South
1♥	1♠	3♥	3♠
4♥	4♠	pass	pass
?			

West needs to re-evaluate his spade holding in the light of the bidding. The point is that the North/South bidding suggests East has at most one spade.

♠ K Q J
♥ A Q 7 5 4 3
♦ K 10
♣ 8 2

With K Q J, West's spade holding will be worth two tricks in defence, but may be wasted in a heart contract. West should double 4♠.

♠ A 3 2
♥ A Q 7 5 4 3
♦ K 10
♣ 8 2

With the ♠A, West should bid 5♥. He has the perfect spade holding opposite a singleton. The missing ♠ K Q J won't matter. His hand is offensive rather than defensive.

standard english system

1 responses to a 1NT opening

Bid	Points	Meaning
2♣	0 upwards Usually 11+	The Stayman convention. Asks opener to rebid a 4-card major, or 2♦ if he doesn't have one.
2♦ 2♥ 2♠	0-10	Sign-off bid. At least five cards in the bid suit.
2NT	11-12	Invitational for 3NT. Opener passes with minimum, or raises to 3NT with maximum.
3♣ 3♦	18+	Looking for a slam in the bid suit. Forcing with at least 5-card suit.
3♥ 3♠	11+	Shows at least five cards in bid suit. Opener rebids 3NT with two or raises with three or more. May be much stronger if interested in slam.
3NT	13-18	Sign-off bid.
4♥ 4♠	11-18	Sign off. Six or more cards in the bid suit.
4NT	19-20	Invitational for 6NT.
5♣ 5♦	14-18	Sign off. Seven or more cards in the bid suit.
5NT	23-24	Asking partner to choose between 6NT with a minimum and 7NT with a maximum
6NT	21-22	Sign-off bid.
7NT	25+	Sign-off bid.
Other slams	19+	Sign-off bids.

2 responses to one of a suit

Response to 1♥	Point count	Description
2♥	6-9 (Limit)	4-card or longer support. (Occasionally only three cards.)
3♥	10-12 (Limit)	4-card or longer support.
4♥	13-15 (Limit)	4-card or longer support.
1NT	6-9 (Limit)	Denies 4 spades. May not be balanced.
2NT 3NT	10-12 (Limit) 13-15 (Limit)	Denies 4 spades, or any 5-card suit.
1♠	6+ (Forcing)	At least four spades, might have a longer minor if fewer than 11 points.
2♣/♦	9+ (Forcing)	At least four cards in the suit.
2♠ 3♣/♦	16+ (Forcing to game)	At least five cards in the suit.

3 values for no trump rebids

	After a one-level change of suit eg, 1♦ – 1♠ – 1NT	After a two-level change of suit eg, 1♦ – 2♣ – 2NT
1NT	15-16 points	–
2NT	17-18 points	15-16 points
3NT	19 points	17-19 points

4 suit rebids by opener

Opener's rebid	Points	Meaning
Opener supports responder's suit.		
1♥ – 1♠ – 2♠	11-14 Limit	4+ spades.
1♥ – 1♠ – 3♠	15-17 Limit	4+ spades.
1♥ – 1♠ – 4♠	18+ Limit	4+ spades.
1♥ – 2♣ – 3♣	11-15 Limit	4+ clubs.
1♥ – 2♣ – 4♣	16+ Limit	4+ clubs.
Opener rebids his own suit.		
1♥ – 1♠ – 2♥	11-14 Limit	5+ hearts.
1♥ – 1♠ – 3♥	15-17 Limit	6+ strong hearts.
1♥ – 1♠ – 4♥	16+	7+ strong hearts.
Opener rebids a third suit below the 'barrier'.		
1♥ – 1♠ – 2♣	11-18	Usually five hearts and 4+ clubs.
Opener rebids a third suit above the barrier (reverses).		
1♥ – 2♣ – 2♠	16+	Always five or more hearts. More hearts than spades.
Opener jumps in a new suit.		
1♥ – 1♠ – 3♣	19+	At least five hearts.

5 opening two-bids

Opening two-bids	Points	Meaning
2♣	23+	Conventional. Game forcing, except 2♣ – 2♦ – 2NT, which shows 23-24 balanced points.
2♦ 2♥ 2♠	N/A	Eight playing tricks. Either a one-suited or two-suited hand. Forcing for one round.
2NT	20-22	Balanced hand. Limit bid.
Over 2♣ the negative is 2♦.		
Over 2♦ /2♥ /2♠ the negative is 2NT.		

6 responses to 2NT

Response to 2NT	Points	Meaning
Pass	0-3	
3♣	4+	Stayman. Asks for 4-card major.
3♦	7+	5-card suit. Game forcing.
3♥/3♠	4+	5-card suit. Game forcing.
3NT	4-10	Sign off.
4♥/4♠	4-10	Sign off. 6-card or longer suit.
4NT	11-12	Invitational to 6NT.
5♣/5♦	6-10	6-card or longer suit.
5NT	15-16	Asking partner to choose between 6NT with a minimum and 7NT with a maximum
6NT	13-14	Sign off.
7NT	17+	Sign off.
Other slams	11+	Sign-off bids.

7 responses to 2♣

Response to 2♣	Points	Meaning
2♦	0-7	Conventional negative bid.
2♥	8+ or	Natural and game forcing.
2♠	ace + king	
3♣		
3♦		
2NT	8+	No suit worth bidding. Game forcing.
3♥	N/A	Solid suit with at least six cards, eg,
3♠		A K Q J 3 2 or A K Q 5 4 3 2
4♣		
4♦		

8 suit overcalls at the one level

Sequence	Meaning of last call
(1♥) – 1♠	5+ spades. Usually 8-16 points.
(1♥) – P – (P) – 1♠	5+ spades. 7-14 points.
1♥ – (1♠) – 2♥	4+ hearts. 6-9 points.
1♥ – (1♠) – 3♥	4+ hearts. 10-12 points.
1♥ – (1♠) – 4♥	4+ hearts. 13+ points or equivalent shape.
1♥ – (1♠) – 1NT	7-9 points. Spade stopper.
1♥ – (1♠) – 2NT	10-12 points. Usually two spade stoppers.
1♥ – (1♠) – 3NT	13+ points. Two spade stoppers.
1♥ – (1♠) – 2♦	9+ points. Forcing.
1♥ – (1♠) – 3♦	16+ points. Five+ diamonds. Game forcing.
1♥ – (1♠) – Dbl	6+ points. Takeout. Four cards in each minor suit.
1♦ – (1♥) – Dbl	6+ points. Takeout with four spades.
1♦ – (1♠) – Dbl	6+ points. Takeout with four hearts.
1♦ – (1♥) – 1♠	5+ spades. 6+ points. Forcing.
1♣ – (1♦) – Dbl	6+ points. Takeout. Four cards in each major suit.
1♣ – (1♦) – 1♥	6+ points. At least four hearts.
(1♥) – 1♠ – (P) – 2♠	3+ spades. 6-9 points.
(1♥) – 1♠ – (P) – 3♠	3+ spades. 10-12 points.
(1♥) – 1♠ – (P) – 4♠	3+ spades. 13+ points.
(1♥) – 1♠ – (P) – 1NT	Two or fewer spades. 9-12 points. At least one heart stopper.
(1♥) – 1♠ – (P) – 2NT	Two or fewer spades. 13-14 points. At least one heart stopper.
(1♥) – 1♠ – (P) – 3NT	Two or fewer spades. 15+ points. At least one heart stopper.
(1♥) – 1♠ – (P) – 2♦	5+ good diamonds. Not forcing.
(1♥) – 1♠ – (P) – 3♦	5+ good diamonds. Forcing.

9 suit overcalls at the two level

Sequence	Meaning of last call
(1♠) – 2♣	Overcall without a jump. 5+ good clubs. 11-18 points. 6+ good clubs. 10-17 points.
(1♥) – P – (P) – 2♣	5+ clubs. 9-16 points.
(1♥) – 2♠	Overcall with a jump. 12-16 points. Good 6-card suit.
(1♥) – P – (P) – 2♠	12-16 points. Good 6-card suit.
1♥ – (2♣) – Dbl	7+ points. Takeout.
1♥ – (2♠) – Dbl	9+ points. Takeout.
(1♠) – 2♥ – (P) – 3♥	3+ hearts. 9-11 points or equivalent in shape.
(1♠) – 2♥ – (P) – 4♥	3+ hearts. 12+ points or equivalent in shape.
(1♠) – 2♥ – (P) – 2NT	Usually two or fewer hearts. 10-12 points.
(1♠) – 2♥ – (P) – 3NT	Usually two or fewer hearts. 13+ points.
(1♠) – 2♣ – (P) – 2NT	10-12 points. Maybe fewer with a good club fit.
(1♠) – 2♣ – (P) – 3NT	13+ points. Maybe fewer with a good club fit.
(1♥) – 2♣ – (P) – 2♠	5+ good spades. Not forcing.
(1♥) – 2♣ – (P) – 3♠	5+ good spades. Forcing.

10 higher level suit overcalls

Sequence	Meaning of last call
(1♥) – 3♠	Pre-emptive. Weak hand with good 7-card suit. Rule of 500.
(1♥) – 3♣	12-16 points. Good 6-card or longer suit.
(1♥) – P – (P) – 3♣	12-16 points. Good 6-card suit.
(1♥) – 4♠	Pre-emptive. Rule of 500, or perhaps stronger and expecting to make.

11 no trump overcalls

Sequence	Meaning of last call
(1♥) – 1NT	16-18 points. Heart stopper.
(1♥) – P – (P) – 1NT	12-14 points. Heart stopper.
(1♥) – 2NT	20-22 points. Heart stopper.
(1♥) – P – (P) – 2NT	20-22 points. Heart stopper.
(1♥) – 3NT	To play. Maybe solid minor suit and heart stopper.
1♥ – (1NT) – 2♥	4+ hearts. 6-9 points.
1♥ – (1NT) – 2♣	5+ good clubs. At most 9 points.
1♥ – (1NT) – Double	10+ points. Any shape.
(1♥) – 1NT – (P) – 2♣	Stayman. Asks for 4-card major (in this case spades).
(1♥) – 1NT – (P) – 2♠	5+ spades. Sign-off bid.
(1♥) – 1NT – (P) – 2NT	7-8 points. Invitational to 3NT.
(1♥) – 1NT – (P) – 3NT	9+ points. Sign-off bid.
(1♥) – 1NT – (P) – 3♠	Five spades. 8+ points. Forcing. Asks for 3-card spade support.
(1♥) – 1NT – (P) – 4♠	6+ spades. Sign-off bid. 8+ points.
(3♥) – 3NT	16+ points with heart stop

12 intervention over 1NT

Sequence	Meaning of last call
(1NT) – Dbl	16+ points. Any shape.
(1NT) – 2♠	5+ good spades. Fewer than 16 points.
1NT – (Dbl) – 2♣	5+ clubs. Sign-off bid. Not Stayman.
(1NT) – Dbl – (P) – 2♣	5+ clubs. Fewer than 5 points.

13 take-out doubles

Sequence	Meaning of last call
(1♥) – Dbl	Takeout. 12+ points.
(1♥) – P – (P) – Dbl	Takeout. 10+ points.
(1♥) – Dbl – (2♥ or 3♥) – Dbl	A takeout double. Denies four spades. 4-4 in the minor suits.
(1♣) – Dbl – (2♣ or 3♣) – Dbl	A takeout double. 4-4 in the major suits.
1♣ – (1♠) – P – (P) – Dbl	Takeout. Short in spades.
1♥ – (Dbl) – Redbl	Short in hearts. 10+ points and hoping to penalise opponents.
1♥ – (Dbl) – 2♥	4+ hearts. 0-5 points.
1♥ – (Dbl) – 3♥	4+ hearts. 6-9 points.
1♥ – (Dbl) – 4♥	4+ hearts. 13+ points or equivalent in shape.
1♥ – (Dbl) – 1NT	Balanced. 7-9 points.
1♥ – (Dbl) – 2NT	4+ hearts. 10-12 points. Conventional and forcing.
1♥ – (Dbl) – 1♠	4+ good spades. Forcing.
(1♥)– Dbl – (P) – 1♠	4+ spades (occasionally three if desperate). 0-8 points.
(1♥) – Dbl – (P) – 2♠	4+ spades. 9-12 points.
(1♥) – Dbl – (P) – 4♠	4+ spades. 13+ points or equivalent in playing strength.
(1♥) – Dbl – (P) – 1NT	6-9 points. Heart stopper.
(1♥) – Dbl – (P) – 2NT	10-12 points. Heart stopper.
(1♥) – Dbl – (P) – 3NT	13+ points. Heart stopper.
(1♥) – Dbl – (P) – P	Very strong hearts. Partner is required to lead a heart if he has one.
(3♥) – Dbl	Takeout, 13+ points

index of key words